Weekend Recipes
Jess Elliott Dennison

Breakfast

Blood Orange Pancakes with forced rhubarb
compote, yoghurt and stem ginger   17

Curry-Butter Eggs on Toast   21

Boiled Eggs with wild garlic soldiers   22

Lemon Curd (for the best toast)   25

Sausage, Apple and Cider-Onion Baguettes   27

Welsh Rarebit, Salad and Cornichons   31

Wholemeal Scones   33

Lunch

Broad Bean, Asparagus and Mint Crostini — 39

Roasted Peppers, Charred Silverskin Onions
and Parmesan (for eating with baguette) — 43

Trout Fishcakes, Green Bean Salad
and Tarragon Mayonnaise — 45

Mackerel Pâté on Crumpets with
really good cucumbers — 49

Salt and Vinegar Roast Potatoes
with Alp Blossom cheese — 51

Herby-Yoghurt Butter Beans
with peas and purple sprouting broccoli — 53

Potato, Parmesan and Oregano Galette
with green salad and cornichons — 55

Roast Chicken and Sage and Onion
Sourdough Stuffing with roast garlic aioli — 59

Chicken, Fregola and Dill Broth — 63

Baked Goat's Cheese and Frisée Salad
with walnuts, honey and chives — 65

Wild Garlic, Farmhouse Cider
and Gruyère Lasagne — 69

Afternoon Baking

Stem Gingerbread Slice ... 75

Fig, Brown Sugar and Oat Cookies ... 77

Fennel Seed Shortbread ... 80

Clementine Eccles Cakes ... 83

Raspberry and Almond Muffins
(that happen to be gluten-free) ... 86

Dinner

Orecchiette with Beef Ragu	91
Sausages with bay and fennel lentils	95
Cider Mussels with rapeseed aioli and baguette	97
Roast Pumpkin and Wine-Braised Beans with artichoke-caper dressing	101
Sage, Hazelnut and Parmesan Linguine	103
Stuffed Tomatoes, Dressed Freekeh and Oregano Yoghurt	106
Spaghetti with Parmesan and Oregano Meatballs	109
Sage, Onion and Wild Mushroom Pie	112
Chicken Curry Pie	115
Crispy Garlic, Cheddar and Spring Onion Mash	119
Braised Olive, Rosemary and Lentil Casarecce	121
Marinated Greens	124

Puddings

Lemon Peel and Bay Custard	129
Blackcurrant Pavlova with elderflower cream and lemon peel and bay custard	133
Lemon Posset	136
Forced Rhubarb and Blood Orange Jelly	139
Flourless Chocolate Cake with crème fraîche and Armagnac prunes	143
Sourdough Summer Pudding	145
Rye Crumb Ice-Cream Cake	147
Cherry and Almond Pudding	151
Apple and Almond Frangipane Galette	153
Coriander Seed Crispbreads for cheese and honey	156

May 2025

Hello. Following on from the success of *Midweek Recipes*, I am delighted to be back with *Weekend Recipes*.

It may be no surprise to hear that I love eating; but I *particularly* love eating and cooking at the weekend. For me, when work is on pause and there's more time available for connecting with my ingredients, kitchen and company – be it friends, family, or even my own thoughts and the song that's playing on the radio – food tastes at its absolute brightest and best.

There's an almost magical quality to the air as time rolls out across the weekend and with it, a distinct relationship to not only what you are eating, but when you are eating it. It therefore felt most natural to structure this second book with chapters of Breakfast, Lunch, Afternoon Baking, Dinner and Pudding.

Breakfast contains the fluffy pancakes that our 3-year-old daughter, Nora, always requests (page 17), and that I like eating with stem ginger and yoghurt. There's also my Curry-Butter Eggs for a livelier take on the usual scrambled eggs (page 21), and a sherbert-y lemon curd for eating on toast (page 25), or even with a batch of my fresh wholemeal scones that have a digestive biscuit-like quality (page 33). Scones for breakfast somehow feels completely acceptable on the weekend.

I've designed the Lunch recipes – see Trout Fishcakes with tarragon mayonnaise (page 45) and the Potato, Parmesan and Oregano Galette (page 55) – to be enjoyed by a couple of you pottering about in the kitchen together. Equally, the same recipes can be scaled up for relaxed hosting when feeding a larger crowd – simply add a green salad, some good baguette and butter, a bottle of wine and you're good to go. These were the kind of dishes that were always popular on my lunchtime menu when I had Elliott's Cafe between 2018-2023 and that I now demonstrate in my Studio, so I'm excited for you to recreate them at home.

I can't not mention the Sunday lunch of Roast Chicken and Sage and Onion Sourdough Stuffing with roast garlic aioli (page 59). It's a fling-it-all-in-one-tray job, including the vegetables, which is ideal for our tiny kitchen. A heavy splash of white wine means the chicken makes its own gravy in the tray, and it's just the thing for soaking up the stuffing, which is inspired by my life-long love of Paxo's sage and onion. You quickly make the aioli by fishing out the garlic that's become all golden and chewy from roasting in the chicken fat, then blitz it with olive oil until really thick – just divine for dipping your juicy chicken, roast potatoes and carrots into. This relaxed Sunday lunch has become the part of my week that I look forward to most as we sit around the table and recalibrate as a little family before the busyness of a new week sets off. Plus, there's usually enough leftovers for making the Chicken, Fregola and Dill Broth on Monday night (page 63), and even a round of sandwiches, too.

Afternoon Baking contains the treats I like to offer with coffee for any friends popping in or, if we're going to their house, for wrapping up in brown paper and string. There's my Fig, Brown Sugar and Oat Cookies (page 77) that I kept portions of in the freezer while heavily pregnant with Percy (now 6 months old!). Even when not pregnant, a cookie eaten warm from the oven on a Saturday afternoon is a truly special thing, so I'm hoping the cookies become part of your weekend ritual, too. The Stem Gingerbread Slice (page 75) is a doddle to throw together and as close as I can get to the famously secret 'Sarah Nelson Grasmere Gingerbread'. The almond-based muffins (page 86) are very much friand/financier in style, and are the ideal canvas for whichever fruit is in season. I serve these as a welcome at any creative workshops running in my Studio. Then there are my flaky-pastry Eccles cakes (page 83), filled with their clementine and lemon sultana caramel filling.

The Dinner chapter is all about comfort, so you'll find pies with homemade buttery pastry (see the Chicken Curry Pie on page 115), satisfying pastas (Sage, Hazelnut and Parmesan Linguine on page 103 and Spaghetti with Parmesan and Oregano Meatballs on page 109), and wine-braised beans, including my favourite white bean dish with big chunks of roasted pumpkin and a punchy artichoke-caper dressing (page 101).

Puddings are a topic I get very excited about (a future book, perhaps?). Mine tend to be quite old-fashioned and not overly sweet, so you'll find nostalgic flavours like rhubarb jelly (page 139), my Sourdough Summer Pudding (page 145) for when the berries are at their best and, of course, my Blackcurrant Pavlova (page 133) with elderflower cream and lemon peel and bay custard. This layered meringue is the most requested pudding from my Studio events, so I'm delighted it's finally getting its place in print.

Talking of print, I'd like to highlight the wonderful team that have helped me bring this follow-up title together. For the past few months, I've been sending out these recipes for testing to an online community of 175 testers, and their dedication to providing insight and feedback makes the recipes as robust as they can possibly be. Collaborating with Glasgow-based designer Maeve Redmond has continued to be such a pleasure, and I know my copy will become an object that I will treasure forever thanks to her thoughtful design and dedication to her craft. My editor, Gemma Hinstridge, has kept me right with all of the words, spelling and grammar. I still don't quite understand the difference between a dash and an en-dash, and I tend to waffle on too much... but thankfully she keeps me right. The work of illustrator Lilly Hedley always makes me smile and I feel so lucky to have her artistic touch in this series, including exploring different flowers from our garden for the covers.

This time last year, I cheekily asked my mum and dad if I could store a few boxes of *Midweek Recipes* in my old bedroom at their house, wondering if anyone would even buy a copy. Since then, Den and Claire have turned that room into the biggest part of Elliott's, receiving pallets of books from our printer, Gomer in Wales, alongside a full online retail collection for the kitchen and home. They post out daily orders across the UK and as far as the USA and Australia, even though they're supposed to be retired! As well as carrying thousands of books up endless steps to Mum and Dad's house, doing late-night ingredient-shopping trips, and delivering boxes of books to local stockists, my husband Philip has been so supportive by taking care of Nora and Percy, enabling me to get my head down on this project.

I get quite teary thinking about how supportive independent retailers have been with my first Elliott's book, and I'm so excited to tour these new recipes, including a big celebratory lunch with the Edinburgh International Book Festival.

Reader, whether it's making lemon curd on toast in your pyjamas on a lazy Sunday morning, or setting the table with your finest plates for an impressive dinner on a Saturday night with friends, I really hope these recipes bring as much joy to your weekends as they do mine.

Jess

Breakfast

Blood Orange Pancakes with forced rhubarb
compote, yoghurt and stem ginger
17

Curry-Butter Eggs on Toast
21

Boiled Eggs with wild garlic soldiers
22

Lemon Curd (for the best toast)
25

Sausage, Apple and Cider-Onion Baguettes
27

Welsh Rarebit, Salad and Cornichons
31

Wholemeal Scones
33

Blood Orange Pancakes with forced rhubarb compote, yoghurt and stem ginger

Blood Orange Pancakes
with forced rhubarb compote, yoghurt and stem ginger

As well as being my daughter's favourite, my community of recipe testers went mad for these fluffy little pancakes and I think it's down to the combination of stem ginger, its glorious syrup and plenty of orange zest.

Forced rhubarb and blood oranges provide the injection of colour we're all craving in the kitchen after a long winter in the UK. Of course, just substitute for other citrus and non-forced rhubarb, or indeed any other soft fruit, when making these pancakes at other times of year.

Makes 14 small pancakes
Takes 20 minutes

STEWED FORCED RHUBARB
1 blood orange or ½ regular orange
2 stems forced rhubarb, sliced into 2cm chunks
4 tbsp caster sugar

PANCAKES
175g plain flour
2½ tsp baking powder
40g caster sugar
1 free-range egg
200ml whole milk
cold-pressed rapeseed oil or vegetable oil
    and salted butter for frying

TO SERVE
200g Greek yoghurt (the really thick stuff)
2 balls stem ginger in syrup, finely sliced
1 blood orange, skin removed and cut into slices

Using a microplane or the fine side of a box grater, zest the blood orange into a large mixing bowl then set aside for the pancake batter as you're going to make that once you've done the compote.

Juice the zested orange then pour the juice into a pan along with the rhubarb, caster sugar and a few splashes of water. Heat on medium for 3–5 minutes or until soft and stewed, then taste for sweetness. I like it quite tart but you may want to add slightly more sugar. Transfer to a bowl and allow to cool.

To make the pancake batter, return to the bowl of orange zest then add in the flour, baking powder, caster sugar and egg. Whisk to combine, then gradually pour in the milk, whisking until you have a pourable batter, the consistency of lightly whipped cream.

Pour a few tablespoons of oil into a large frying pan on a high heat, then use a piece of kitchen paper to ensure the surface is well greased. Add a tiny knob of butter to the pan, reduce the heat to medium then add small spoonfuls of batter to the pan, allowing for room around each pancake. Cook for 1–2 minutes, or until bubbles begin to surface on each pancake, then carefully flip and cook for a further 1–2 minutes until golden and fluffy.

Carefully remove the pancakes from the pan, grease the surface with the oiled kitchen paper, add slightly more butter, then repeat with the remaining batter.

Serve up the pancakes with the stewed rhubarb, blood orange slices, Greek yoghurt and sliced stem ginger.

NOTES
+ Use up any leftover stem ginger for the chewy, biscuity slice on page 75.
+ You can of course use regular rhubarb if you can't get hold of forced rhubarb the colour won't be as striking, but it will still be really delicious.

Blood Orange Pancakes with forced rhubarb compote, yoghurt and stem ginger

Curry-Butter Eggs on Toast

Curry-Butter Eggs on Toast

A hot mug of tea and these curry-butter eggs is such a great way to start the weekend, and I'm imagining you have most of the ingredients already to hand.

You're aiming for a folding technique rather than a traditional homogeneous scramble for the eggs, so a rubber spatula comes in handy when cooking them.

Takes 10 minutes

PER PERSON
1 slice white sourdough bread
¼ red or green chilli
few sprigs coriander or parsley
1 tbsp cold-pressed rapeseed oil or light olive oil
1 tbsp (15g) butter (salted or unsalted)
½ tsp curry powder
½ tsp garam masala
3 free-range eggs
sea salt flakes
¼ lemon

Pop your bread in the toaster. Preheat a medium frying pan on medium-high then, using a sharp knife, finely chop the chilli and coriander, including the stalks.

Place the oil, butter and spices in the hot pan and stir until lightly foaming, then reduce the heat to low and crack in the eggs with a good pinch of salt. Using a wooden spoon or spatula, gently fold the eggs for a minute or so (rather than stirring like mad) until silky and cooked through. You should end up with beautiful folds of cooked egg rather than a homogeneous scramble.

Plate up the toast (I don't bother buttering it as the egg mixture is so rich), top with the eggs, chopped chilli, and herbs. Using a microplane, zest over the lemon then squeeze over the juice.

Boiled Eggs with wild garlic soldiers

If I was ever poorly as a little girl, Mum would make me 'dippy egg and soldiers'. It was deeply comforting, so when the wild garlic appears in our garden at the start of spring, this is the first thing I make with it. Marmite, my Dad's favourite, or anchovy on salted-butter soldiers also works a treat at other times of the year.

Makes 8 servings of butter
Takes 15 minutes

WILD GARLIC BUTTER
1 handful wild garlic, washed and dried
200g salted butter, softened
pinch sea salt flakes
1 tbsp extra virgin olive oil

PER PERSON
2 medium free-range eggs
1 slice good bread for toasting
tiny wedge lemon
(anchovies in oil and chilli flakes to serve, optional)

To make the butter, finely slice the wild garlic then add to a large bowl along with the softened butter, salt and oil. Using a wooden spoon (and lots of elbow grease!) or a handheld electric whisk, beat until fully combined.

Boil your eggs in a pan of boiling water for 6½ minutes (this should give you cooked whites and soft, dippable yolks). Toast your bread then slather with the garlic butter and a squeeze of lemon, then cut into soldiers. Top with a few anchovies and some chilli flakes if they're your thing, then get dipping.

NOTES
+ The butter will keep in the fridge for a week or so if well wrapped in greaseproof paper or cling film.

Boiled Eggs with wild garlic soldiers

Lemon Curd (for the best toast)

Lemon Curd (for the best toast)

It's no secret that I'm a big fan of all things citrus, and I find that half a grapefruit and the tiniest pinch of sea salt join forces to make the most sherberty, lemony version of this addictive curd.

Assuming you have decent bread, this lemon curd really does make for the best toast. The other opportunities for its use are near endless: over hot crumpets, onto scones with clotted cream (see page 33) with shop-bought vanilla ice-cream, as a layer in a trifle and even on a giant pavlova (see page 133).

Makes 2 × small (220g) jars
Takes 20 minutes

1½ lemons
½ grapefruit
100g butter (salted or unsalted)
teeny-tiny pinch sea salt flakes
100g caster sugar
2 free-range eggs
really good bread for toast

Set aside 2 small jars or a medium glass bowl. (If you plan on keeping the curd for a while or gifting a jar then you'll need to sterilise the jars thoroughly, though we never find we need to as the curd disappears so quickly in our house!).

Using a microplane or the fine side of a box grater, zest the lemons and grapefruit. Squeeze their juice until you have 100ml lemon and grapefruit juice in total, discarding any pips. Place the zest, juice, butter, salt and sugar into a bowl sitting over a small pan of gently simmering water, allow it to melt, then stir until the sugar dissolves and it's no longer grainy in texture.

Crack in the eggs, then whisk to combine into the melted butter mixture. Keep an eye on the heat as you don't want scrambled eggs – low and slow is the best approach when making curd.

Whisk regularly for 5–10 minutes or until thick enough to coat the back of a wooden spoon (bear in mind that the curd will continue to thicken as it cools). Pour into the jars/bowl, then allow to cool completely before storing in the fridge. Slather the curd on hot toast for a brilliant start to your day.

NOTES

+ If kept in clean jars, the curd will keep happily in the fridge for up to 2 weeks.
+ You can pass it through a sieve for an extra smooth curd before pouring into jars if you like, but I never bother as it's delicious as is.
+ Swap the lemons and grapefruit for limes, oranges or, if you're lucky enough to get hold of one, bergamot. Just aim for 100ml citrus juice in total.
+ If you want an impressive pudding for entertaining, the madeleines from *Midweek Recipes* served with the curd, some gently whipped cream and fresh cherries or raspberries could be a good idea. Or even with the meringues on page 133.

Sausage, Apple and Cider-Onion Baguettes

A sausage sandwich after hours of dance classes is how I spent Saturday mornings as a little girl, and years on I still think it's one of the best things you can eat. My taste buds have become slightly more sophisticated as I've aged, so the sliced white wonderloaf is now a sourdough baguette and the silly amount of tomato ketchup has been replaced with slices of apple cooked down with sage, onions and cider until sweet and sticky. The essence of this magnificent breakfast remains the same, however. Perhaps it's time to dust off those tap shoes?!

Makes 2 hefty portions
(or could also feed 3 less greedy people)
Takes 35 minutes

1 tsp fennel seeds
black pepper
400g good-quality pork sausage meat
   (roughly 6 sausages)
3 tbsp cold-pressed rapeseed oil or light olive oil
2 onions, finely sliced
½ tsp salt
1 apple (any variety you fancy)
5g sage leaves (roughly 10 large leaves)
200ml dry cider (or apple juice)
1 large good-quality baguette
Dijon mustard and wholegrain mustard, to serve

First, preheat the oven to 200°C (400°F/gas 6). Line a large baking tray with greaseproof paper.

Crush the fennel seeds in a pestle and mortar (or with a rolling pin on a board), then transfer to a mixing bowl along with a good few grindings of black pepper. Remove the sausage meat from the skins then, using wet hands, mix with the fennel seeds and pepper until evenly distributed. Flatten the sausage meat into 2 long patties on the baking tray, aiming for 1cm depth and the same width as your baguette. Bake for 20 minutes, or until the sausage meat is golden on the outside and cooked through in the centre.

Meanwhile, heat the oil in a large pan on a high heat, add in the onions and salt then allow the onions to start gaining colour and catch at the edges slightly – this should take 6-8 minutes and you only need to stir occasionally. Slice up the apple into thin 'half moons' (don't bother peeling the apple, but do discard the core). Add the apple and sage to the pan and fry for 3-4 minutes so that the apple starts to lightly brown and the sage releases its scent. Pour in the cider then simmer for 5 minutes on a high heat or until you get a reduced, deliciously sticky mixture.

Slice the baguette open lengthways, leaving one seam-edge intact (so the fillings don't fall out later), then liberally spread with Dijon mustard and wholegrain mustard, top and bottom. Layer up the cooked sausage patties followed by the apples and onions then cut into 2 or 3 portions, depending on how many you're feeding. Eat straight away while everything is still warm.

NOTES
+ If you've got any in the fridge, a handful of watercress or rocket would make a lovely fresh addition.
+ I don't bother buttering the baguette as there's plenty of fat in the sausage mixture, but feel free to pour any cooking juices from the sausage tray onto the baguette before spreading with mustard. Delicious.

Sausage, Apple and Cider-Onion Baguettes

Welsh Rarebit, Salad and Cornichons

Welsh Rarebit, Salad and Cornichons

This requires slightly more effort than straight-up cheese on toast, but it's just so comforting, especially in the colder months. The cheese and stout béchamel-like mixture needs to sit and continue to thicken for at least 15 minutes, so I like to prepare this element, go for a long, brisk walk, then return to the enjoyable task of grilling oozy slices of the rarebit to eat with cornichons and a perfectly dressed salad.

Makes 4 hefty slices or 6 smaller slices
Takes 20 minutes, plus 20 minutes cooling time

20g butter (salted or unsalted)
1½ tbsp plain flour
100ml Guinness or stout
¾ tsp English mustard powder
½ tsp Dijon mustard
¼ tsp Worcestershire sauce, plus extra to taste
150g mature Cheddar cheese, grated
4 large slices white sourdough
cornichons or pickled silverskin onions, to serve

SALAD
½ tsp Dijon mustard
1 tbsp cold-pressed rapeseed oil or light olive oil
pinch caster sugar
tiny pinch sea salt flakes
¾ tsp cider vinegar or white wine vinegar
½ butterhead or another type of nice lettuce
    (chicory, rocket or watercress also works well)

First, place the butter in a medium pan on a low-to-medium heat, allow it to melt, then add in the flour. Using a wooden spoon, stir for a minute or two, until the butter has absorbed the flour and is smelling nutty and biscuity and slightly darkening in colour.

Add the stout, English mustard powder, Dijon mustard, Worcestershire sauce and cheese to the pan and keep stirring for a few minutes until you get a smooth, béchamel-like sauce that coats the back of your wooden spoon. Transfer to a deep tray or dish and allow to cool, thicken and set enough so that it's spreadable for the toast. This will take at least 15–20 minutes, but you can do it hours or even days in advance.

When you're ready to eat, whisk the salad dressing ingredients in a large bowl and have a taste for seasoning. Tear in the leaves so that they retain some beautiful, natural shape, and toss to dress.

Set your grill to high then lightly toast both sides of the bread. Spread the cheese mixture over one side of each slice, then grill until oozy and blistering. Serve with the salad, plenty of cornichons and the bottle of Worcestershire sauce.

NOTES
+ I don't tend to drink stout, so I freeze 100ml portions for using at a later date to prevent wastage.
+ You can keep the cheese mixture in the fridge where it will sit very happily for up to 5 days, so it's handy for whipping up for a quick midweek dinner.

Wholemeal Scones

They might not win a prize for their looks, but this is my favourite way to scone as the touch of wholemeal flour and brown sugar gives them a lovely digestive biscuit-like quality. When I can find it, beremeal (ancient barley) flour from Barony Mill, the last working water mill up in Orkney, is my go-to flour, but add any wholemeal that you've got to hand.

Eat these fresh from the oven if you can, and it goes without saying that clotted cream, good jam or lemon curd (see page 25) are essentials.

Makes 6 small scones (plus a cook's taster)
Takes 10 minutes, plus 14 minutes baking time

150g plain flour, plus extra for dusting
75g wholemeal flour (spelt and rye are my faves)
2 tsp baking powder (level, not heaped teaspoons)
30g light brown sugar
tiny pinch sea salt flakes
50g cold butter (salted or unsalted)
1 free-range egg
50–100ml milk
(1 tsp rolled oats, optional)

First, preheat the oven to 200°C (400°F/gas 6), then line a baking tray with greaseproof paper.

Weigh out the flours, baking powder, sugar and salt in a large bowl then whisk with a fork to ensure the baking powder is well distributed. Add the cold butter in small cubes, then rub in with your fingertips until the mixture resembles fine breadcrumbs.

Crack the egg into a measuring jug, add enough milk to make the total liquid up to 150ml, then whisk to combine. Add most of the egg and milk mixture into the flour and stir until you get a soft dough. You may not need all of the egg-milk mixture so go canny: it's better to add in stages rather than make the mixture too wet. Any leftovers can be used to glaze the top of the scones.

Turn out the dough onto a lightly floured work surface, knead lightly, then roll out to a rectangle about 2cm thick.

Using a biscuit cutter or glass, cut out six 6cm rounds plus an ugly little 'cook's treat scone' with the scraps, then place on the lined baking tray. Lightly brush the tops of the scones with a little extra milk, or any egg and milk left in the jug, and sprinkle with oats if you like.

Bake for 12–14 minutes, or until the scones are well risen and a pale, golden-brown colour. They should sound hollow if you tap their bases.

Serve straight away with butter, jam, clotted cream, lemon curd... or all of the above!

NOTES
+ A fresh scone is the best kind of scone; but once the scones are cool, they can be frozen. To eat, defrost at room temperature and then reheat in a hot oven for 10 minutes.
+ As there's a digestive-biscuit quality to these scones, they're delicious served with a strong Cheddar or your favourite crumbly cheese and fresh grapes.

Wholemeal Scones

Lunch

Broad Bean, Asparagus and Mint Crostini
39

Roasted Peppers, Charred Silverskin Onions
and Parmesan (for eating with baguette)
43

Trout Fishcakes, Green Bean Salad
and Tarragon Mayonnaise
45

Mackerel Pâté on Crumpets
with really good cucumbers
49

Salt and Vinegar Roast Potatoes
with Alp Blossom cheese
51

Herby-Yoghurt Butter Beans
with peas and purple sprouting broccoli
53

Potato, Parmesan and Oregano Galette
with green salad and cornichons
55

Lunch

Roast Chicken and Sage and Onion Sourdough
Stuffing with roast garlic aioli
59

Chicken, Fregola and Dill Broth
63

Baked Goat's Cheese and Frisée Salad
with walnuts, honey and chives
65

Wild Garlic, Farmhouse Cider
and Gruyère Lasagne
69

Broad Bean, Asparagus and Mint Crostini

I hadn't planned on including this crostini recipe, but I was writing this book at the same time as hosting my Spring Series 2025 where this was the welcome snack. Everyone kept asking for the recipe so I've snuck it in.

The different shades of green from the beans, asparagus, peas and mint work so elegantly together here. You may be a little surprised by how much good olive oil I've used, but it really makes them, so go with me. A few of these – as they are, or served with a farmhouse cheese or some lightly cured ham – makes for a really good lunch, especially when paired with an organic white or rosé wine as we did in my Studio.

Makes 20 crostini
Takes 30 minutes

1 good-quality baguette
   (I like a sourdough one)
150g frozen petit pois
200g frozen broad beans (skin-on weight)
125g asparagus
zest of 1 lemon, plus 1¼ tbsp lemon juice
1¾ tsp sea salt flakes
tiny pinch chilli flakes
¼ tsp fennel seeds, crushed
5 tbsp extra virgin olive oil,
   plus 4 tbsp for the baguette
5 sprigs mint (roughly 18g)
125g sauerkraut (drained weight), finely sliced

First, preheat the oven to 200°C (400°F/Gas 6). Slice the baguette into 1.5cm-ish slices, then lay them on a baking tray. You should get around 20 or so slices. Bake for 8–10 minutes, flipping halfway through until golden at edges but still slightly soft in the middle. Remove from the oven and turn it off.

Meanwhile, boil the kettle then place the peas and broad beans in a pan and cover with boiling water for 1–2 minutes, or until defrosted enough that you can handle the broad beans to remove their skins. You shouldn't need to turn the heat of your stove on as such. Drain the peas and broad beans in a colander then remove and discard all the broad bean skins. Transfer to a large bowl.

Bring a small pan of water and 1 tsp salt to the boil, then snap the asparagus stems to remove their woody ends. Boil the asparagus for 1–2 minutes (depending on how thick the stems are), then drain in a colander and rinse under plenty of cold water to keep the asparagus' vibrant colour. Slice into ½ cm rounds.

Using a microplane, zest the lemon into the bowl of peas and broad beans then add the lemon juice, ¾ tsp salt, the chilli flakes, crushed fennel seeds and 5 tbsp oil. Pick in the mint leaves (discard the stalks) then, using a hand blender, gently blitz until you get a rough, crushed texture, as per the photo. (You're looking to keep some of the pea and broad beans whole and recognisable.) Stir in the sliced asparagus then have a taste for seasoning, you may want extra salt and lemon.

Drizzle the slices of baguette with plenty of olive oil (roughly 4 tbsp!), then place a small amount of sauerkraut on each slice. Using a teaspoon, smoosh a generous amount of the pea mixture onto each crostini. You can zest over extra lemon if you like, too.

NOTES
+ It's not essential of course, but if they're in your garden, a few wild garlic flowers make a beautiful garnish for the crostini.

Broad Bean, Asparagus and Mint Crostini

Roasted Peppers, Charred Silverskin Onions and Parmesan (for eating with baguette)

Roasted Peppers, Charred Silverskin Onions and Parmesan (for eating with baguette)

A quick char in the oven brings new life to a jar of silverskin onions in this recipe, and by silverskin onions I don't mean anything special – just an old-fashioned jar of regular pickled onions, you know, the kind that were very popular eaten with cocktail sticks in the 1970s.

There's hardly any hands-on cooking here, just really good ingredients working well together and lots of roasting juices asking to be mopped up with baguette. I'm thinking of these peppers, a cold bottle of white wine and a big salad for a Saturday afternoon catch-up with a friend at our kitchen table.

Serves 2
Takes 15 minutes, plus 30 minutes roasting time

2 red or orange pointed peppers
    (sadly, green ones don't work for this)
3 garlic cloves
pinch chilli flakes
¼ tsp sea salt flakes
a few grindings of black pepper
3 tbsp extra virgin olive oil, plus extra to serve
8 silverskin onions from a jar
½ a good quality fresh baguette,
    cut into 2cm thick slices
tiny wedge of lemon
45g Parmesan (or Pecorino/Grana Padano) cheese

First, preheat the oven to 200°C (400°F/Gas 6) then line a baking tray with greaseproof paper.

Slice the peppers in half lengthways, remove any seeds, then place cut-side up on the tray. Peel and slice the garlic as finely as you can, then scatter the slices over the peppers along with the chilli flakes, salt and pepper. Drizzle with the oil (I know it's a generous amount of oil, but you're going to mop up the delicious oily juices with slices of baguette soon).

Cover the tray with foil (this is important as you don't want the garlic to burn). Pat the onions dry with kitchen paper then place on top of the foil (it might feel weird doing this, but go with me!). Roast for 30 minutes or until the onions are charred and the peppers are completely juicy and tender.

Allow the peppers and onions to cool slightly so that you can handle them, then tear the peppers into long strips and cut the onions into halves. Pile onto the slices of baguette with a squeeze of lemon juice then, using a speed peeler, shave over the cheese. Spoon over any tray juices (and finish with an extra drizzle of oil if you like, too).

NOTES
+ If anchovies are your thing, replace the sea salt with a few tinned anchovies to season the peppers instead. You get such a beautiful umami hit to contrast with the sweet roasting juices.
+ You could make a big batch of this and it'll sit very happily in the fridge when covered in oil, so great for getting ahead when hosting.

Trout Fishcakes, Green Bean Salad and Tarragon Mayonnaise

When blind-testing these fishcakes, my friend Erin wrote: *"They generally reversed everything I thought I knew about fishcakes (peeled large potatoes, smooth mash, mash must be fridge cold, fish must be gently poached, breadcrumbs)."* So I'm sharing this insight so you know what to expect.

As much as I love a classic breadcrumbed fishcake (ideally from the chippy!), the mixture here of skin-on potatoes and raw, fresh trout results in a fishcake that is much more rustic and fresh.

Keep the method for dressing the green beans up your sleeve for other meals too: the lightly pickled shallot vinaigrette means they're great as a side dish in their own right.

Serves 2, makes 4 large fishcakes
Takes: 45 minutes

FISHCAKES
325g baby potatoes (don't peel them)
sea salt flakes
100g green beans
4 spring onions
15g flat-leaf parsley
1 free-range egg
1 lemon
2 sustainably sourced trout fillets (approx 250g)
2 tbsp plain flour
vegetable oil, light olive oil or sunflower oil
    for frying
1 tbsp natural yoghurt
2 tbsp mayonnaise
    (from a jar, or use the aioli recipe from page 97)
1 tbsp finely chopped tarragon leaves

GREEN BEAN SALAD
1 tbsp lemon juice
½ banana shallot or very small onion, finely sliced
1 tsp cider vinegar or white wine vinegar
½ tsp Dijon mustard
1 tbsp extra virgin olive oil
pinch sea salt flakes
pinch caster sugar
½ tbsp capers

First, halve the potatoes then place them in a medium pan with ½ tsp salt and cover with plenty of water. Bring to the boil over a high heat then simmer for 20 minutes. Trim the beans then add to the pan, and simmer for a further 3–4 minutes until tender. Drain the beans and potatoes in a colander.

Transfer the beans to a large bowl then, using a fork or potato masher, crush the potatoes in the pan until you get a rough mash. Finely slice the spring onions, roughly chop the parsley (discard any really tough stalks) then place them in the pan of mash. Crack in the egg, then using a microplane or the fine side of a box grater, zest in half of the lemon. Tear away and discard the skin from the trout fillets, cut the fish into 1cm chunks, then add to the pan along with ¾ tsp salt (this feels like lots of salt; but I promise the cooked fishcakes won't taste overly salty). Thoroughly mix until everything is nicely combined then place the flour on a plate. Form the mixture into 4 large fishcakes (roughly 3cm in thickness), and coat well in the flour.

To cook the fishcakes, place enough oil in a wide pan to give you a thin layer for frying, then place on a high heat for 45 seconds so that it's really hot. Carefully place the fishcakes in the pan then reduce the heat to medium-high and fry for 3–4 minutes on one side until a deep golden brown. (It's tempting to prod and poke; but try not to interfere with the fishcakes until 3–4 minutes is up so that they don't fall apart.) Using a fish slice, flip and cook

Trout Fishcakes, Green Bean Salad and Tarragon Mayonnaise

for another 3–4 minutes on the other side, again, until a deep golden brown. Remove the pan from the heat and transfer to a plate lined with a sheet of kitchen paper to absorb any excess oil.

While the frying is happening, return to the bowl of green beans, toss in all the dressing ingredients, then stir to coat.

In a small bowl, stir together the yoghurt, mayonnaise and chopped tarragon with a teeny-tiny pinch of salt. Cut any remaining parts of unjuiced lemon into wedges.

To serve, divide the fishcakes between 2 plates, pile up the green beans, dollop on the tarragon mayo and finish with the lemon wedges for squeezing over.

Mackerel Pâté on Crumpets with really good cucumbers

Mackerel Pâté on Crumpets
with really good cucumbers

If you like the sound of the flavours going on in the fishcakes on the previous page but don't have enough time for boiling the potatoes and frying etc, then this is the recipe for you.

Once made, the pâté will sit very happily in the fridge for a few days, so it's great for getting ahead if you've got people coming over. It also works really well as a starter for a dinner party or at Christmas. If you're eating the pâté with crumpets, which I recommend, just promise me you will get them really well toasted first – you're looking for some crunch to contrast with the smooth mackerel.

Makes 6 crumpets
Takes 20 minutes

CUCUMBERS
Takes 5 minutes

½ shallot or ¼ white onion (15g)
½ tbsp capers
zest of ¼ lemon and 2 tsp lemon juice
2 tsp cold-pressed rapeseed oil or olive oil
½ tsp white vinegar
tiny pinch fennel seeds
tiny pinch chilli flakes
tiny pinch caster sugar
pinch sea salt flakes
100g cucumber
    (use baby cucumbers if you can find them)
1 tbsp torn dill fronds or a few tarragon leaves

MACKEREL PÂTÉ
3 fillets of sustainably sourced smoked mackerel
    (200g)

35g butter (salted or unsalted), room temperature
2½ tbsp Greek yoghurt (the really thick stuff)
black pepper
6 crumpets, to serve

First, make the cucumbers so that they have a chance to marinate. Peel and finely slice the shallot, then add it to a bowl along with the capers, lemon zest and juice, oil, vinegar, fennel seeds, chilli flakes, sugar, and salt. Slice the cucumber into thin rounds and tear the dill, then throw them into the dressing.

To make the pâté, remove and discard the skin from the mackerel. Tear big chunks of the fillets and throw them into a food processor along with the butter and yoghurt. Grind in loads of black pepper then pulse until fully combined but still rough in texture. (You could do all of this by hand if you don't have a food processor.)

When you're ready to eat, toast the crumpets until really deep golden brown and crisp. Spread over the pâté then load up with the cucumbers, ensuring you spoon over the cucumber dressing.

Salt and Vinegar Roast Potatoes with Alp Blossom cheese

I first made these potatoes for my Spring Series in 2024 and they've been a constant in my kitchen ever since as everyone goes mad for them. They're essentially mini baked potatoes drenched in butter, good vinegar, lots of sea salt and melted mountain-style cheese – all good things! I'm hoping these little potatoes will quickly become part of your weekend repertoire too, either offered on a big platter as a welcome snack to serve with drinks, or with a few slices of ham and a green salad for a leisurely lunch.

Alp Blossom is a very special cheese. The cheesemakers rub the mix of wild flowers and herbs that the cows graze on over the rind, so it not only looks pretty but also makes for a wonderfully aromatic cheese. Of course, substitute for something like Comté or Gruyère from your local supermarket if Alp Blossom is proving too tricky to get hold of.

Serves 4 as a hefty snack
Takes 1 hour

1kg baby potatoes (washed and dried if muddy)
1 tbsp extra virgin olive oil
    or cold-pressed rapeseed oil
sea salt flakes
150g Alp Blossom cheese (or Comté, Gruyère)
3 tbsp good quality cider vinegar
    or white wine vinegar
35g butter (salted or unsalted)

First, preheat the oven to 200°C (400°F/Gas 6) then place the potatoes on a large baking tray so that they sit in a single layer (I use the tray that came with the oven). Rub the oil all over the potato skins then sprinkle

Salt and Vinegar Roast Potatoes with Alp Blossom cheese

over plenty of sea salt. Roast for 45 minutes, tossing the tray halfway through until the potatoes are really deep golden, crispy on the outside and super soft and fluffy on the inside. Turn the oven off.

Meanwhile, use a speed peeler to shave the cheese into thin slices.

Using a really sharp knife, and taking care as they're piping hot, slit the potatoes open (as if they are mini jacket potatoes), then sprinkle plenty of salt into the fluffy insides along with the vinegar. Dot the butter into each potato then stuff with the shavings of cheese.

Eat straight away while still warm or, if you like, return the tray to the oven for a minute or two so that the cheese melts in the residual heat. So indulgent, so delicious!

Herby-Yoghurt Butter Beans
with peas and purple sprouting broccoli

I've adapted this recipe from my first book, *Salad Feasts*, that I wrote back in 2018, as all these years on it's still such a good go-to for those occasions when you're asked to bring a big salad or side dish to a barbecue, picnic or 'pot luck'.

Try and stretch to a jar of really good quality butter beans rather than tinned beans here (Bold Bean Co. and El Navarrico are both great) as it makes all the difference to the final dish. Purple sprouting broccoli has a fairly short season, so swap for regular broccoli, green beans or asparagus if they're easier to source.

Serves 4
Takes 15 minutes

350g purple sprouting broccoli
    or Tenderstem broccoli
300g frozen petits pois
100g pine nuts
1 × 700g jar queen butter beans,
    rinsed and drained
2½ tbsp capers, roughly chopped
20g Parmesan or pecorino cheese

DRESSING
125g natural yoghurt
½ small garlic clove
1 small bunch (15g) basil
1 small bunch (15g) dill
1 small bunch (15g) mint, leaves only
1½ tbsp extra virgin olive oil
¼ tsp sea salt flakes
zest and juice of ½–1 lemon

Herby-Yoghurt Butter Beans with peas and purple sprouting broccoli

First, bring a medium pan of water to the boil. Trim the ends off the broccoli then blanch for 3 minutes over a high heat until vibrant green. Remove with a slotted spoon, rinse under cold water then drain in a colander and set aside. Add the peas to the boiling water and cook for 1–2 minutes, rinse under cold water and drain completely.

Next, toast the pine nuts in a dry frying pan over a high heat for 2–3 minutes until lightly golden and releasing their natural oils. Pine nuts can burn easily, so stir frequently and keep an eye on them. Transfer to a plate and set aside to cool.

To make the dressing, blitz half the peas with the yoghurt, garlic, herbs, oil, salt and zest and juice of half the lemon in a food processor. Have a taste – you may want to squeeze in the other lemon half – then transfer to a large mixing bowl. Toss in the butter beans, remaining peas, toasted pine nuts, capers and broccoli.

Using a microplane or fine side of a box grater, grate over the cheese to finish.

Potato, Parmesan and Oregano Galette
with green salad and cornichons

Galettes are a kind of free-form tart that feature heavily in my weekend cooking as they're so relaxed yet satisfying. For the minimal effort this pastry recipe requires, you are rewarded with a flaky, buttery crust that serves as a base for whatever toppings you fancy. There's no worrying about lamination or the precise shaping of the dough; in fact, the rougher your galette, the more rustic and inviting it will end up looking.

I find less is more when it comes to toppings and there's something beautifully simple about how the potato, garlic, Parmesan and oregano work together here. I'm spoiled for oregano as my husband grows loads in our garden then dries it out for me to use throughout the year. It's worth seeking out a big bunch of dried stuff from your local deli if you can as it's got much more flavour than the supermarket jars.

Serves 6 with a green salad for lunch, or 4 for dinner
Takes 15 minutes, plus 1 hour chilling time
and 1 hour baking time

PASTRY
150g plain flour, plus extra for dusting
tiny pinch sea salt flakes
85g cold butter (salted or unsalted), cut into cubes

FILLING
40g Parmesan cheese
5 garlic cloves
350g waxy baby potatoes
½ tsp dried oregano
¾ tsp sea salt flakes
3 tbsp extra virgin olive oil
black pepper
½ tbsp milk

SALAD
½ tsp Dijon mustard
1 tbsp extra virgin olive oil
tiny pinch caster sugar
tiny pinch sea salt flakes
¾ tsp cider vinegar or white wine vinegar
½ butterhead, frisée, or another type of nice lettuce
cornichons, to serve

First, make the pastry dough. Rub the flour, salt and butter together in a large bowl, using your index and middle fingers and thumbs, until you've got large, rough flakes. Don't worry if some of the butter remains quite chunky.

Stir in a few splashes of cold water then mix with your hands until combined to a soft dough. Wrap it in cling film and pop in the fridge for at least 1 hour, or in the freezer for 30 minutes.

Once the pastry has chilled, preheat the oven to 200°C (400°F/Gas 6). Lay a sheet of baking paper on your work surface and lightly dust it with flour. Roll out the pastry to a rough circle, about 28cm in diameter, on the floured paper. You can use a rolling pin or even a wine bottle to do this, and don't worry about the pastry circle being perfectly round or neat at the edges. In fact, the scruffier the shape, the better.

Transfer the pastry circle – still on the paper – to a large baking tray. Using a microplane, finely grate over a layer of Parmesan, leaving a roughly 2cm clear border all the way round. (Only use up half of the Parmesan as you want some for the top, too.) Peel and slice the garlic as finely as you can, then scatter over the pastry.

Slice the potatoes as finely as you can then place a layer of potatoes over the Parmesan. Sprinkle over half the oregano, half the salt and half the oil; then repeat with a second layer of potatoes, oregano, salt and oil. Finely grate over the remaining Parmesan and plenty of black pepper, then fold the edges of the pastry inwards to overlap the filling, pinching it slightly to create a crust.

Potato, Parmesan and Oregano Galette

Using a pastry brush, dab the crust with milk and bake in the preheated oven for 25 minutes, by which time it should be deep golden brown. Reduce the oven to 180°C and bake for a further 15 minutes to ensure a really flaky base and crust, but without it burning, then remove from the oven.

Whisk together the salad dressing ingredients in a large bowl and have a taste for seasoning. Tear in the leaves so that they retain some beautiful, natural shape and toss to dress. Cut the galette into slices and serve with the dressed leaves and plenty of cornichons.

Roast Chicken and Sage and Onion Sourdough Stuffing with roast garlic aioli

Roast Chicken and Sage and Onion Sourdough Stuffing with roast garlic aioli

As we have such a tiny kitchen to keep two little people entertained in while cooking, this is my answer to the perfect Sunday lunch with comfort and interest but none of the stress. You essentially throw the whole chicken and all of the vegetables onto a single tray with lots of garlic, thyme and wine then allow the oven to do all the hard work, including making a zesty little gravy. You're then freed up to make a really good stuffing: the flavours here are heavily inspired by a box of Paxo's sage and onion (a life-long obsession of mine!), plus a quick aioli blended with the slow-roasted garlic that you can then dip your chicken-fat potatoes into – it's heavenly stuff.

The bonus of this roast is that any leftovers can be simmered together in a pot the next day to give you the most nourishing bowl of broth for adding small pasta like fregola, orzo or even broken spaghetti to. See the full method on the next page.

Serves 4
Takes 25 minutes, plus 1 hour roasting time

1 garlic bulb, cut in half through the equator
6 shallots (don't bother peeling them), halved
20g fresh thyme
4 carrots, peeled, cut into 4cm chunks
750g baby potatoes
   (don't bother peeling or chopping them)
1 large free-range chicken (approx 1.6kg)
1 lemon
3 tbsp cold-pressed rapeseed oil or olive oil
sea salt flakes
black pepper
250ml white wine
(blanched green beans, peas or broccoli to serve,
   optional)

SOURDOUGH STUFFING
1 onion, finely chopped
8 sage leaves, roughly sliced
1 tbsp cold-pressed rapeseed oil or olive oil
30g butter (salted or unsalted)
pinch sea salt flakes
180g white sourdough, blitzed into breadcrumbs
1 free-range egg

ROAST GARLIC AIOLI
75ml sunflower oil or vegetable oil
25ml extra virgin olive oil
1 tsp Dijon mustard
1 free-range egg

Take your chicken out of the fridge 20 minutes before you start cooking to bring it closer to room temperature before roasting. Preheat the oven to 200°C (400°F/gas 6) and prepare the vegetables as per the ingredients list.

Line your largest tray with greaseproof paper (I use the tray that came included with our oven). Place the garlic, shallots and thyme (don't bother picking it) in the centre of the tray and the carrots and baby potatoes around the outside of the tray. Place the chicken in the centre then cut the lemon in half. Squeeze both lemon halves over the skin then push them inside the cavity. Drizzle the bird and veg with the oil, then season with plenty of salt and pepper. Roast for 30 minutes.

Meanwhile, make the stuffing by frying the onion and sage in the oil, butter and salt in a pan on a low-to-medium heat for 15 minutes until softened. Remove from the heat and allow to cool for 5–10 minutes. Using a food processor, blitz the sourdough into breadcrumbs then stir into the slightly cooled onions along with the egg until fully combined.

Remove the chicken from the oven, toss the vegetables (these should be nicely caramelised at the edges by this point), then reduce the temperature to 180°C (350°F/

gas 4). Pour the wine into the base of the tray then blob the stuffing on top (you could make little stuffing balls if you like but I go for the rustic approach). Roast for a further 25–40 minutes or until the chicken juices run clear when you insert a sharp knife into the leg joint. The timing will be determined by the size of the bird, so it's best to check the leg area as this takes the longest time to cook. Allow the chicken to rest for a few minutes while you make the aioli.

Once it's cool enough to handle, squeeze all of the garlic out of its skins into a jug, large jar, or the plastic beaker that comes included with your hand blender. Add in the oils, mustard and egg then blitz with a hand blender for 30 seconds to 1 minute, by which time you should have a beautifully thick aioli. (Have a taste of the tray gravy then taste the aioli for seasoning; I find the white wine is zingy and salty enough that the aioli doesn't need extra lemon or salt, but see what you think.)

Carve up the chicken then plate up along with the veg, stuffing (and any extra greens). Using a spoon, scrape any sticky bits from the bottom of the tray into the white wine gravy then spoon over each plate along with a blob of aioli.

Chicken, Fregola and Dill Broth

Chicken, Fregola and Dill Broth

Fregola is a small, round, Sardinian pasta that is rolled, sun-dried and toasted. A single bag contains distinct shades of yellows, golds and browns, so if you see it in your local deli then buy a bag or two for throwing in fridge-raid soups or leftover roast chicken broths such as this one.

I've used a large handful of dill and a tin of cannellini beans for adding to the chicken broth here as they are staples in our kitchen, but the spirit of this dish is to use up what is to hand, so any soft herbs or cooked beans will do. If fregola is proving too difficult to find, orzo, broken spaghetti or indeed any odds and ends of pasta packets from the back of the cupboard will work well.

Serves 4–6
Takes 20 minutes, plus 2½ hours simmering time

1 tbsp sea salt flakes, plus extra to taste
2 onions, skin-on, roughly chopped
100g fregola (orzo and broken spaghetti also work well)
1 × 400g tin cannellini beans, drained
20g dill (or any soft herbs)
1 lemon
extra virgin olive oil
black pepper
Roast garlic aioli (see page 60)

Once you've enjoyed your roast from page 59, transfer the carcass and any leftover vegetables into a large pot (with a tight-fitting lid). Make sure you scrape any jellied tray juices into the pot as these are full of flavour, but remove the lemon as it can make your broth overly bitter. Add the salt and fresh onion, keeping the skins on the onions as that will turn your broth golden.

Cover with 3 litres of boiling kettle water then bring to

the boil. Reduce to a simmer then pop the lid on and let it simmer away for 2 hours. Remove the lid and simmer for a further 30 minutes to reduce slightly. Have a taste for salt: you may want slightly more, depending on what you're planning on adding to your broth.

Sit a large colander over a second large pan or bowl then carefully pour the broth into the colander. (I tend to do this in the sink so that it creates less mess to wipe up). Once cool enough to handle, pick off any good bits of chicken or vegetable to add to the broth then discard the rest.

Meanwhile, cook the fregola in a small pan of boiling water for 10–12 minutes, or until al dente, then drain in a large sieve.

Gently heat the broth then throw in the cooked fregola and beans, and taste for seasoning. Divide between bowls then tear over the dill. Using a microplane, zest over the lemon, then drizzle over the olive oil. Finish by cracking over plenty of black pepper. If you have any leftover roast garlic aioli from page 60 then this is delicious dolloped on top too.

Alternatively, allow the broth to cool and freeze in small portions so that you're covered for great chicken stock when a recipe calls for it.

NOTES
+ If you want a new batch of aioli for serving with the broth but don't have any leftover roast garlic, just make using ⅓ raw peeled garlic clove, 75ml sunflower oil or vegetable oil, 25ml extra virgin olive oil, 1 tsp Dijon mustard, 1 free-range egg and a squeeze of lemon juce as per the hand blender method on page 60.
+ A few handfuls of something green is a great addition to this soup; finely sliced cavolo nero, spring greens or even some peas from the freezer all work well.

Baked Goat's Cheese and Frisée Salad with walnuts, honey and chives

This pleasing French bistro-style salad is so incredibly easy to throw together and exactly the kind of thing I want to eat whilst catching up with a friend after a busy week.

As it's going to be baked, you're looking for an individual rind-on goat's cheese, or a thick slice from a log with the rind still intact, so don't pick up the soft, mousse-like rindless variety by mistake.

I love the texture and slight bitterness that frisée brings to this salad, but of course, you can substitute for butterhead, chicory or baby gem. Likewise, the walnuts can be swapped for pecans or hazelnuts, just roast them gently first as the oven warms up if they've been sitting in the cupboard for a while.

Serves 2
Takes 15 minutes

100g rind-on soft goat's cheese
1 tsp Dijon mustard
2 tsp cider vinegar
1⅓ tbsp extra virgin olive oil
2 tbsp natural yoghurt
tiny pinch sea salt flakes
black pepper
80g frisée lettuce
4 sprigs chives (flowers picked if with flowers)
50g walnuts or pecans
1 tsp good-quality honey
(sourdough baguette to serve, optional)

First, preheat the oven to 200°C (400°F/gas 6). Line a small baking tray with greaseproof paper. Place the cheese on the tray then bake for 10 minutes, by which point the inside should be melted. Remove from the oven.

Meanwhile, stir the mustard, vinegar, oil, yoghurt, salt and a few turns of black pepper together in a large mixing bowl. Throw in the frisée lettuce then roughly chop and throw in the chives (plus any chive flowers if you're lucky enough to have those). Using your hands, crush in the walnuts then toss everything to coat in the dressing. Have a taste for seasoning then divide the dressed salad between 2 plates.

Slice the baked goat's cheese in half (taking care as it will be molten-like in the middle) then sit it on the plates of salad. Drizzle over the honey then serve straight away (with slices of baguette too, if you like).

Baked Goat's Cheese and Frisée Salad with walnuts, honey and chives

Wild Garlic, Farmhouse Cider and Gruyère Lasagne

Wild Garlic, Farmhouse Cider and Gruyère Lasagne

Here, fresh pasta sheets (easier to make than you might think) are layered with a farmhouse cider, Gruyère and Parmesan cheese sauce, and wilted wild garlic — the majestic ingredient that for me marks spring's arrival to my kitchen more than any other.

Although there are a few elements to prepare, everything is therapeutic to do, can be made well in advance and is easily scaled up for feeding a larger crowd. You can of course make the lasagne with dried pasta sheets if fresh dough is a step too far, and when wild garlic is out of season spinach with a little grated garlic can be used. If using dried pasta sheets, just bear in mind that they will absorb more moisture than fresh pasta when baking, so aim for a slightly looser béchamel.

Serves 2 generously
Takes 1 hour 30 minutes, plus 1 hour pasta dough resting time and 30 minutes baking time

FRESH LASAGNE SHEETS
100g plain or 'tipo 00' flour, plus extra for dusting
1 free-range egg

BÉCHAMEL SAUCE
35g salted butter
3½ tbsp plain flour
¼ tsp sea salt flakes
150ml whole milk
250ml dry farmhouse cider
50g Gruyère cheese, grated
25g Parmesan cheese, grated

WILD GARLIC PESTO
20g wild garlic (or 20g flat-leaf parsley
   and ½ garlic clove, peeled)

20g basil
20g Parmesan cheese
10g panko breadcrumbs
2 tbsp extra virgin olive oil
zest of 1 lemon
2 tsp lemon juice

WILTED GREENS
25g wild garlic (or 25g extra spinach and
　1 garlic clove, peeled and crushed)
75g spinach
1 tbsp extra virgin olive oil
pinch sea salt flakes

To make the fresh lasagne sheets, place the flour on your work surface then make a little well to crack the egg into. Use a fork to whisk the egg, gradually bringing in the flour, then use your hands to knead into a smooth, silky dough. (You may need to dust your hands and work surface with flour a few times until the dough stops feeling sticky).

Wrap the dough in cling film then pop in the fridge to rest for an hour (or overnight).

To make the béchamel, place the butter in a medium pan then heat on high to melt it. Stir in the flour and salt then cook out for a further 2 minutes on high, stirring regularly. Pour in the milk, a few splashes at a time, stirring regularly until you get a thick paste. Reduce the heat to medium then add the cider in stages until you get a thin sauce. Throw in the cheeses then reduce the heat to low, allow the cheese to melt, and stir until you get a thick, smooth sauce. Set aside.

To make the pesto, wash the wild garlic then drain in a colander and place in a small food processor along with the other pesto ingredients, then blitz until smooth. Set aside.

For the wilted greens, wash the wild garlic and spinach then drain in a colander. Heat the oil in a large frying

Wild Garlic, Farmhouse Cider and Gruyère Lasagne

pan then add the greens and salt and fry on high for 2–3 minutes until wilted. Set aside to cool slightly.

When ready to assemble and bake, remove the rested pasta dough from the fridge then, using a rolling pin or pasta machine, roll out the dough into thin sheets to fit your chosen dish.

Preheat the oven to 200°C (400°F/gas 6). Spoon a thin layer of béchamel sauce over the base of the dish, then add a lasagne sheet, another thin layer of white sauce, a few tiny blobs of pesto and a few wilted greens. Repeat the layers until you've used up the lasagne sheets. Finish with a final layer of béchamel sauce and a few blobs of pesto.

Bake for 20–25 minutes, or until bubbling and beginning to catch on top and at the edges.

Serve up with a green salad tossed with a punchy viaigrette or the green beans from page 45.

Afternoon Baking

Stem Gingerbread Slice
75

Fig, Brown Sugar and Oat Cookies
77

Fennel Seed Shortbread
80

Clementine Eccles Cakes
83

Raspberry and Almond Muffins
(that happen to be gluten-free)
86

Stem Gingerbread Slice

Stem Gingerbread Slice

From one simple dough you get three textures in this addictive gingerbread slice: crunchy biscuit on the bottom, a chewy, treacly middle and a crumble-like topping. It's inspired by Victorian cook Sarah Nelson and her famous Grasmere Gingerbread that she created in 1854 and which is still made by hand at her original Lake District kitchen today (worth a visit if you're ever in the area).

Sarah's recipe is top secret, but with lots of testing I reckon I'm pretty close to the original... with my addition of stem ginger, which is one of my favourite things to bake with. The best thing about this recipe is just how ridiculously easy it is. You simply add everything to a food processor (or you can mix with your hands in a bowl), pop the dough into a lined baking tray then brown in the oven for a few minutes. Just the thing to have up your sleeve for those moments when you're in need of something sweet.

Makes 15 pieces
Takes 10 minutes, plus 20 minutes baking time

115g butter (salted or unsalted), cut into cubes, plus extra for greasing
225g plain flour
115g light brown sugar
1 tsp ground ginger
pinch sea salt flakes
2 balls jarred stem ginger in syrup (45g), roughly chopped
2 tbsp black treacle

First, preheat the oven to 180°C (350°F/gas 4) and use a tiny bit of butter to grease a brownie tin or square cake tin. The one I use is 20 × 26cm but don't worry too much about the size. Line with greaseproof paper then set aside.

The best way to make the mixture is in a food processor with the sharp blade attachment. Pulse the butter, flour, sugar, ground ginger and salt until you get fine breadcrumbs. Add the stem ginger (not any syrup) and treacle, then pulse again until evenly distributed.

Press all but 75g of the mixture into the lined tin, pressing down hard. Sprinkle the remaining 75g over the top to form a 'crumble-style' topping. Bake for 20 minutes, allow to cool for 3–4 minutes, then slice up while still warm as it will continue to firm up as it cools.

Enjoy slightly warm or cool.

NOTES

+ You can still make this if you don't have a food processor; simply rub the butter, flour, sugar, ground ginger and salt together between your fingers in a large bowl until you get fine breadcrumbs. Finely chop the stem ginger and mix into the breadcrumbs with the treacle. This is a sticky but easy job to do and your finished slices will look more rustic, but still taste delicious.

Fig, Brown Sugar and Oat Cookies

As great as a classic chocolate chip cookie is, I'm sometimes looking for something more interesting from a tray of homemade cookies, and that's where these come in. Grinding a few turns of black pepper into the dough subtly brings out the flavour of the figs, which may sound slightly strange, but do trust me.

I love how the brown sugar adds a caramel-like flavour without making the cookies overly sweet. They're especially good when eaten warm from the oven so I highly recommend freezing balls of the dough then baking them off fresh whenever you're in the mood for one. These cookies are also brilliant for sandwiching good quality vanilla ice-cream. Enjoy!

Makes 8 large cookies
Takes 15 minutes, plus 15 minutes freezing time
and 20 minutes baking time

110g plain flour
¼ tsp bicarbonate of soda
pinch sea salt flakes
80g porridge oats
black pepper
85g dried figs, finely sliced into rounds
125g butter (salted or unsalted), softened
100g light brown sugar
50g caster sugar
1 free-range egg yolk
    (use the whites for the pavlova on page 133)

First, line a small tray or tupperware with greaseproof paper and make space for it in your freezer.

Weigh out the flour, bicarb, salt and porridge oats in a large bowl. Grind in a few turns of black pepper (sounds odd for a cookie, but trust me!) then stir with a fork to ensure the bicarb is well distributed. Stir in the sliced figs

Fig, Brown Sugar and Oat Cookies

ensuring you discard any stalks as they can be very hard to eat once baked.

Place the butter, brown sugar and caster sugar in another large bowl then, using an handheld electric whisk (or a wooden spoon and lots of elbow grease!), beat until just combined. Crack in the egg yolk and mix again. Don't worry if it looks slightly curdled, just stir in some of the flour from the other bowl.

Stir the dry ingredients into the butter mixture until you have a dough. It will feel quite sticky compared to, say, a chocolate chip cookie dough, but that's correct, don't worry.

Divide into 8 balls, roughly 70g each, then pop onto the lined tray and freeze for at least 15 minutes.

Meanwhile, preheat the oven to 180°C (350°F/gas 4) and line 2 large baking trays with greaseproof paper (the cookies will spread quite a bit, so leave plenty of room). Bake for 18–20 minutes or until golden and crisp at the edges. Allow to cool on the tray where they will continue to crisp up as they cool.

NOTES

+ You can make the whole batch of dough then just bake off a few cookies at a time as they keep perfectly in the freezer. Just leave them out at room temperature for 5 minutes before baking if you've had them in the deep-freeze for a while.
+ These keep well in an airtight container for 3 days after baking.

Fennel Seed Shortbread

It's true. I have a fennel seed addiction! I just find they add a little aniseedy magic to so many of my recipes and this shortbread is no different. A slice of this shortbread is particularly good alongside the blackcurrant fool that you'll find in my *Midweek Recipes* book.

A lot of trouser-tightening recipe testing has gone into perfecting the shortbread texture for you here, so I encourage you to use it as your shortbread blank canvas. The fennel seeds can easily be swapped for citrus zest, Earl Grey tea or crushed cardamom seeds. Have a play with different flavours including any forgotten spice jars from the back of your cupboard.

Makes 12 slices
Takes 15 minutes, plus 40 minutes baking time

1 tsp fennel seeds, plus ½ tsp for topping with
125g cold salted butter, cut into small cubes
60g light brown sugar
145g plain flour
30g cornflour
½ tsp caster sugar

First, preheat the oven to 160°C (325°F/gas 3).

Line an 18cm round cake tin with a square of greaseproof paper. I find the easiest way to do this is by scrunching the paper into a ball, unfolding it, then securing into place by clipping it to the side of the tin with metal clips.

Crush 1 tsp fennel seeds in a pestle and mortar, or with a rolling pin on a board.

In a large bowl, rub the butter, brown sugar, plain flour, cornflour and crushed fennel seeds between your fingers until you have a very fine breadcrumby texture. Tip into the lined tin then, with your fingers or the base of a cup, push down really hard to compress the mixture.

Fennel Seed Shortbread

Bake for 35–40 minutes, or until deep golden, taking care not to burn the shortbread. (You might want to keep an eye on it for the last 10 minutes.)

Very importantly, while it's still warm and therefore easy to slice, cut into 12 slices then sprinkle with the caster sugar and a few extra fennel seeds. Allow to cool fully, or do as I do and sneak warm pieces from the tin as it's cooling.

NOTES
+ The baked shortbread keeps well in a tin or tupperware for a week or so. You can also keep the raw dough in the fridge for a day before baking if you're getting ahead for people coming over.
+ Have a play with other spices such as cardamom and cinnamon, or even some finely chopped dark chocolate.

Clementine Eccles Cakes

Clementine Eccles Cakes

One shouldn't pick favourites in a book, but if you wanted to know which baking recipe I recommend you try first then it would be these. The clementine zest, juice and garam masala brings a tutti frutti-like quality to a traditional Eccles filling and achieving your own bakery-standard flaky pastry is truly satisfying.

I will be making these year-round from now on, adapting the filling slightly to suit the season. At the start of the year and up until Easter I'll swap the clementine for blood orange and serve them with clotted cream, as I did at my Spring Series 2025. As we hit the colder months and especially in the run up to Christmas, a splash of rum or whisky will make its way into the filling and they'll be served instead of mince pies alongside a slice of Anster or Caerphilly cheese. My friend, the potter Cara Guthrie, has even thrown us 'the Eccles plate' specially for serving these on.

Makes 10
Takes 20 minutes, plus 1 hour chilling time and 20 minutes baking time

PASTRY
110g plain flour, plus extra for dusting
75g cold butter, cut into cubes (salted or unsalted)
tiny pinch sea salt flakes

FILLING
40g butter (salted or unsalted), cut into cubes
100g soft brown sugar (dark or light)
165g sultanas (or raisins/currants)
1 tsp garam masala
a few grindings black pepper
zest and juice of 1 clementine
    (to give you about 30ml juice)
zest of 1 small lemon

TOPPING
2 tbsp milk
1½ tbsp Demerara sugar (the visibly crunchy type; don't substitute for anything more refined)

First, rub the flour, butter and salt together in a large bowl, using your index and middle fingers and thumbs until you've got a fine breadcrumby texture. Stir in a few splashes of cold water, then gently mix with your hands until the mixture is combined to a dough.

Wrap the dough in cling film then rest in the fridge for at least half an hour (and up to 24 hours if you're getting ahead).

Meanwhile, for the filling, place the butter, sugar, sultanas, garam masala and black pepper in a small pan. Using a microplane or the fine side of a box grater, zest the clementine and lemon then add to the pan along with the juice of the whole clementine. Place on a medium heat and stir for 2–3 minutes until the butter and sugar is melted and everything is nicely combined. Remove from the heat and set aside to cool.

Preheat the oven to 180°C (350°F/gas 4). Line a large baking tray with greaseproof paper.

Remove the dough from the fridge 5 minutes before you roll out so that's it not rock solid. Lightly dust your work surface with flour then, using a rolling pin, roll out the dough to a rectangle roughly 3mm in thickness and 57cm × 24cm in length. Cut the rectangle in half lengthways, then into 5 widthways, to give you 10 squares.

Place a tablespoon of the sultana filling into the centre of each square then pull up the sides of the pastry to cover the filling. Squeeze to seal each Eccles cake with your fingers, then turn it over and gently squish down until about 5.5cm in diameter.

Brush the tops of the cakes with milk and sprinkle with the sugar. Using a sharp knife, make a few tiny incisions in each. Transfer them to the lined tray and bake for 18–20 minutes until a deep golden brown. Move the baked

Clementine Eccles Cakes

Eccles cakes with a spatula or fish slice to a plate while still warm so that they don't glue themselves to the tray with the melted sugar or any leaked filling.

You can eat these warm from the oven, or allow them to cool and enjoy with a strong cup of tea.

Raspberry and Almond Muffins
(that happen to be gluten-free)

Made from melted butter, egg whites and ground almonds, these are very much friand or financier in style, so really squidgy and light and unsurprisingly they disappear rather quickly in our house. You simply fling everything into a bowl then give the batter a mix before spooning into muffin cases and baking.

As the batter is gluten-free, the muffins keep in perfect condition without drying out for 3–4 days and you can of course swap the raspberries for blackberries, rhubarb, blackcurrants etc as the seasons roll out. Whole, skin-on almonds that you slice up yourself bring an added texture to the tops of these, but use pre-flaked almonds if you prefer.

Makes 10 muffins
Takes 10 minutes, plus 25 minutes baking time

50g salted butter
230g caster sugar
180g ground almonds
30g cornflour
zest of ½ orange
zest of ½ lemon
4 free-range egg whites
   (save the yolks for the custard on page 129)
120g raspberries
40g almonds (ideally skin-on)
(1 tbsp icing sugar for dusting, optional)

First, preheat the oven to 180°C (350°F/gas 4). Line a muffin tin with 10 paper muffin cases.

Place the butter in a small oven-proof dish (I use an enamel bowl), then pop it in the oven to melt as the oven heats up. Remove the now-melted butter from the oven

Raspberry and Almond Muffins

then carefully pour it into a large mixing bowl. Throw in the sugar, ground almonds, cornflour, orange zest, lemon zest and egg whites then whisk to combine.

Spoon the batter into the muffin cases then top with a few raspberries on each. Slice up the almonds then scatter over. Bake for 22–25 minutes until the muffins are deep golden in colour. Remove from the oven and allow them to cool completely. (Using a small sieve, dust with the icing sugar.)

Dinner

Orecchiette with Beef Ragu
91

Sausages with bay and fennel lentils
95

Cider Mussels with rapeseed aioli and baguette
97

Roast Pumpkin and Wine-Braised Beans
with artichoke-caper dressing
101

Sage, Hazelnut and Parmesan Linguine
103

Stuffed Tomatoes, Dressed Freekeh
and Oregano Yoghurt
106

Spaghetti with Parmesan and
Oregano Meatballs
109

Sage, Onion and Wild Mushroom Pie
112

Dinner

Chicken Curry Pie
115

Crispy Garlic, Cheddar and
Spring Onion Mash
119

Braised Olive, Rosemary and Lentil Casarecce
121

Marinated Greens
124

Orecchiette with Beef Ragu

I have such fond memories of making this beef ragu for a birthday party in my Studio a few years ago with Phoebe Moon, my creative assistant and gorgeous friend. Heavily influenced by her Greek heritage and London upbringing, Phoebe is simply one of the best cooks I've had the pleasure of working with.

It was Phoebe's idea to use a hand blender to very lightly blitz the slowly-simmered ragu we had prepared before tossing it through the cooked pasta along with generous handfuls of grated Parmesan. Thanks to the blender and a good splash of milk, our beef ragu became more like an incredibly delicate veal ragu, so this is the method I'll be doing for life now.

A word of warning though: don't get over excited with the blender, a few pulses is all you need for the perfect, soft texture. Any more than that and you could end up with soup!

Serves 8, so you can make a big batch then freeze half
Takes 30 minutes, plus 1 hour simmering time

2 carrots, peeled
1 large onion
1 stick celery
3 tbsp extra virgin olive oil
2 tsp sea salt flakes, plus extra for the pasta water
40g butter (salted or unsalted)
3 bay leaves
tiny pinch chilli flakes
¼ tsp fennel seeds
½ tin sustainably sourecd anchovies
    (about 5 fillets)
750g beef mince (ideally at least 15% fat)
2 garlic cloves
2 tbsp tomato purée
350ml milk (ideally whole)

300ml white wine
1 × 400g tin plum tomatoes
orecchiette, or your favourite pasta
Parmesan cheese, for finely grating

Roughly chop the carrots, onion and celery then place in a food processor and blitz until really fine, almost a paste (or dice as finely as you can). Add the blitzed veg along with the oil, salt, butter, bay leaves, chilli flakes, fennel seeds and anchovies to a large saucepan then heat on a medium-high heat for 10 minutes or so, stirring regularly. You're aiming for everything to go golden, as if you were cooking out a curry paste.

Add the beef mince to the pan, increase the heat to high and allow it to brown, caramelise and break down for 4–5 minutes. As you're stirring everything with a wooden spoon, you should find that the anchovies are breaking down and almost disappearing by this stage.

Using a microplane, mince the garlic into the pan and allow it to cook out for 2–3 minutes until fragrant, but not burning. Stir in the tomato purée then cook it out for 2 minutes, stirring regularly. Pour in the milk, wine and tomatoes, bring to the boil, then reduce to a simmer with a lid on. (Don't panic if it looks quite oily or if the milk looks slightly curdled at the top of the pan at this point.)

Simmer for 1 hour, stirring the pot every 20 minutes or so to check that nothing's sticking to the bottom of the pan. Remove from the heat then fish out the bay leaves. Using a hand blender, very gently pulse the ragu 2 or 3 times to get it really soft. TAKE CARE and go canny with the blender: you don't want soup! Have a final taste for seasoning, bearing in mind that you're going to add Parmesan and some salted cooking water.

WHEN YOU'RE READY TO EAT

Measure out 100g orecchiette per person and cook until al dente in plenty of salted boiling water, making sure you reserve a mugful of the starchy water. Finely grate

Orecchiette with Beef Ragu

a few large handfuls of Parmesan, depending on how many of you are eating. Drain the pasta in a colander then, in the same pan you cooked the pasta in, heat up a few ladlefuls of the ragu, a few splashes of cooking water and the Parmesan. Keep stirring and tasting until you reach your idea of perfection, then serve up. Extra gratings of Parmesan on top are always a good idea too!

NOTES

+ As with anything tomato-sauce based, something magical happens if you leave this to sit in the fridge overnight, so if you have time, make it the day before eating. It's still incredible on the day, though.
+ Any leftovers can be portioned up and frozen for enjoying up to a month later.

Sausages with bay and fennel lentils

Sausages with bay and fennel lentils

This is my idea of a good, proper supper for when the evenings start to get colder and darker and you're in need of a bit of comfort. The sausages could be served with mash, of course (see page 119 for my dream mash setup), but to me, well-prepared lentils are a really beautiful thing; nourishing and filling but not so rich that you can't handle pudding.

The key to perfect lentils is starting them off in a pan of cold water with plenty of bay leaves that you then bring up to a simmer so that the outsides don't go mushy whilst waiting for the insides to cook, which is what can happen if you throw the lentils directly into boiling water. The required cooking time will be dependent on age and variety, so keep tasting regularly for 'done-ness'. Tender is the aim.

Serves 4
Takes 55 minutes

225g dried green or puy lentils
4 bay leaves
8 good-quality pork sausages
1 carrot
1 onion
1 fennel
2 tbsp extra virgin olive oil
25g butter (salted or unsalted)
½ tsp sea salt flakes, plus extra to taste
3 sprigs thyme
2 fat garlic cloves
100ml white wine
1½ tsp Dijon mustard, plus extra for the table

First, place the lentils and bay leaves in a large pan then top up with plenty of cold water. Bring to the boil then reduce the heat and simmer for 25 minutes, or until tender but cooked through. Drain in a colander then discard the bay leaves.

Meanwhile, preheat the oven to 180°C (350°F/gas 4) and line a baking tray with greaseproof paper for the sausages. Roast for 25 minutes, turning halfway until golden and cooked through – you could also grill them if you prefer.

While the sausages are cooking, peel and finely dice the carrot and onion. Remove the fronds from the fennel (you want to save these for serving later), then finely dice the fennel bulb. Heat the oil and butter in a large frying pan on a high heat then add the chopped carrot, onion and fennel with the salt. Pick in the thyme leaves (discard the stalks) and fry on high for 15 minutes, stirring occasionally. Once the veg is softened, reduce the heat to medium-low, then peel, bash and finely slice the garlic before adding it to the pan. Fry for a further 5 minutes, stirring regularly so that the garlic doesn't burn. Once everything is really sticky and tasting sweet, add the wine, drained lentils and mustard. Allow the lentils to cook on low for 2–3 minutes (by which time they should have absorbed the wine) then have a taste, you may want extra seasoning.

Divide the lentils and sausages between 4 plates, then tear over the fennel fronds for garnish.

Cider Mussels with rapeseed aioli and baguette

Having small children means I don't get to do the long wine-filled bistro lunches I so often fantasise about. But if I make these mussels with garlicky aioli and good crusty baguette then close my eyes for a moment... I'm right there, back in France as a twenty-something!

Please don't be scared by the thought of cooking mussels. They are surprisingly quick and easy to prepare yet always feel like such a treat. Just follow my guidance below on cleaning them and you'll be good to go.

Serves 2 very generously
Takes 35 minutes

MUSSELS
1kg fresh, sustainably sourced mussels
25g butter (salted or unsalted)
2 banana shallots, peeled and finely sliced into 'half moons'
3 fat garlic cloves, peeled and finely sliced
3 sprigs thyme, leaves picked
pinch sea salt flakes
150ml dry cider
½ lemon
10g flat-leaf parsley, finely chopped
½ good-quality baguette to serve, cut into 2cm slices

QUICK AIOLI
25ml extra virgin olive oil
75ml cold-pressed rapeseed oil
1 free-range egg
½ small garlic clove, peeled
1 tsp Dijon mustard
tiny pinch sea salt

First, prepare and clean the mussels by plunging them in a large bowl of really cold water sitting in the sink. Sorting through, one-by-one, pull away any beards – the little threads that the mussel attaches itself to a rock or rope in the sea with – they aren't very pleasant to eat.

Once the mussels are de-bearded and have sat in the cold water for at least 5 minutes, check to see if they're all still healthy and alive by ensuring their shells have closed. If there's a mussel that is open, tap it firmly on the side of the bowl for a few seconds – if it is alive, it will close. Throw away any mussels that refuse to close their shell or that have a broken shell.

Next, make the aioli by placing both oils, the egg, garlic, Dijon mustard and salt in a narrow, tall, vessel – something like a jug, large jar, or the plastic beaker that comes included with your hand blender. Blitz with a hand blender for 30 seconds to 1 minute, by which time you should have a beautifully thick aioli. (I would usually taste for seasoning at this point, but I'd recommend seeing how the mussel cooking juices taste first before you tweak the aioli.) Transfer to a small serving bowl.

When you're ready to cook the mussels, heat the butter until melted in a pan that has a lid and is large enough to fit the mussels with plenty of room so they can soon steam. Add the sliced shallot, sliced garlic, thyme leaves and a tiny pinch of salt then fry on a medium heat for 3–4 minutes, stirring regurly until golden but not catching as you don't want the garlic to burn.

Drain the mussels in a colander then tip them into the pan. Crank the heat up to high, then pour in the cider, pop on the pan lid and allow to steam-cook for 5 minutes or so, until all the shells have opened. Discard any mussels with shells that refuse to open.

Using a microplane, zest the lemon into the pan then squeeze in a little juice. Throw in the parsley then give the mussels a good stir. Taste the pan juices: you may want to add more lemon or salt. Go back to the aioli and see if you'd like to tweak that too to balance with the mussels.

Cider Mussels with rapeseed aioli and baguette

Take the pan of mussels to the table along with the aioli and baguette, then tuck in.

NOTES
+ You can of course substitute the cider for white wine, I just love the depth of flavour and slight sweetness that dry cider brings.
+ Fries with mussels are always a good idea but I'm too lazy to fry them at home and enjoy dunking with crusty baguette just as much. If you wanted potatoes though, the baked baby potatoes on page 51 would make good starchy sponges for soaking up the delicious mussel cooking juices.

Roast Pumpkin and Wine-Braised Beans with artichoke-caper dressing

Roast Pumpkin and Wine-Braised Beans
with artichoke-caper dressing

When the interesting varieties of squashes and pumpkins like Red Kuri and Crown Prince start arriving at our local greengrocers each autumn, the first thing I want to make with them is this.

Roasting the pumpkin in generous wedges (as opposed to stingy cubes) until slightly charred at the edges not only looks inviting, but really intensifies their sweetness. It's then simply a case of using the best of your store-cupboard to build additional layers of flavour and texture to further elevate the pumpkin. Jarred white beans braised with garlic, thyme and white wine feel almost habitual for me, as does this punchy dressing made from marinated artichokes, capers, parsley and lemon for spooning over.

As there are so many delicious juices to mop up with this meal, I highly recommend some crusty bread for serving alongside, something like a sourdough baguette is ideal.

Serves 4
Takes 50 minutes

1 small Red Kuri squash or Delica pumpkin (roughly 850g)
4 tbsp extra virgin olive oil
½ tsp sea salt flakes
2 fat garlic cloves
2 sprigs thyme
1 × 700g jar of white beans
50ml white wine
100g jarred artichoke hearts in olive oil
2 tsp capers
10g flat-leaf parsley
½ lemon
white sourdough or crusty baguette to serve

First, preheat the oven to 200°C (400°F/gas 6). Remove the stalk and base from the pumpkin then cut in half to scoop out and discard the seeds. Cut the pumpkin into thick wedges then place on a baking tray large enough for the wedges to sit in a single layer (this is because you want the pumpkin to roast, rather than steam).

Drizzle over 2 tbsp oil, toss to coat, sprinkle over the salt then roast for 35–45 minutes, tossing half way through. You're looking for the pumpkin to be completely tender in the middle and starting to catch and caramelise at the edges. Turn off the oven, but keep the pumpkin inside to keep it warm.

Meanwhile, peel the garlic, crush it with the side of your knife then roughly slice. Pick the thyme leaves and discard the woody stalks. Heat the sliced garlic, thyme leaves and the remaining 2 tbsp oil in a wide pan on a low-medium heat for 3–4 minutes, stirring regularly with a wooden spoon.

Pour in the beans (and the jar juices), ensuring you crush the last few beans with your hands (this will make the sauce lovely and creamy). Add the wine then crank up the heat to high and simmer for 10–15 minutes, stirring occasionally until creamy rather than soupy. Have a taste for seasoning: the bean juice may be salty enough to season. Remove from the heat.

Slice up the artichokes into thin wedges (not so fine that they lose their shape and beauty), then place in a small bowl. Crush and roughly chop the capers (again, don't go too fine). Roughly chop the parsley then add to the artichoke bowl along with the capers. Stir to combine. You should find that the oil the artichokes were in is enough to dress the capers and parsley.

Divide the beans between 4 bowls or plates, top each with a few pumpkin wedges then spoon over the artichoke mixture along with any pumpkin-infused oil from the baking tray. Using a microplane, zest over the lemon, then squeeze a few drops of juice over each plate to finish. Serve with plenty of bread for mopping up.

Sage, Hazelnut and Parmesan Linguine

Sometimes, the best dinners after a busy week are simply about putting great ingredients together so that you can then go and flop on the sofa. All the ingredients here are really good friends and hopefully easy for you to get hold of: hazelnuts, pasta, lemon, garlic, Parmesan, sage, nutmeg, butter and good olive oil.

The trick is to get your hazelnuts really deep golden in the oven before starting the sauce as this will give your pasta a restaurant-quality depth. Toss in some cavolo nero or spinach if you need a bit of greenery. For me, though, this is all about the joy of delicious, beige tones.

Serves 2
Takes 25 minutes, plus 15 minutes baking time

50g blanched hazelnuts
sea salt flakes
200g dried linguine
½ lemon
3 fat garlic cloves
50g Parmesan cheese
whole nutmeg for finely grating
30g butter (salted or unsalted)
2 tbsp extra virgin olive oil
10g sage leaves

First, preheat the oven to 200°C (400°F/gas 6), then place the hazelnuts on a baking tray and pop in the oven for 15 minutes or so while it heats up. You want the hazelnuts to turn a really deep golden colour and to smell deeply toasted, but take care not to burn them. Remove from the oven and turn it off.

Transfer the hazelnuts to a large pestle and mortar and lightly crush them (use a rolling pin and bowl if you don't have a pestle and mortar).

Meanwhile, bring a medium pan of water to the boil

Sage, Hazelnut and Parmesan Linguine

on a high heat and throw in plenty of sea salt to season the water. Add the linguine to the pan, stir regularly to prevent the strands sticking to each other, then check it a few minutes before the pack instructions suggest. You want it al dente – which usually takes around 8–10 minutes.

Prepare the sauce ingredients while the pasta cooks. Use a speed peeler to create strips of lemon (aiming for the yellow peel; not so much the white bitter pith) then finely slice. Peel, crush and finely slice the garlic. Finely grate the Parmesan and plenty of nutmeg, around 10 gratings.

In a large frying pan, melt the butter and oil on a medium heat. Throw in the sliced lemon peel and tear in the sage leaves then fry for 2–3 minutes, stirring regularly until they're starting to crisp up. Reduce the heat to medium-low, then add the garlic and hazelnuts and cook for a further couple of minutes until the garlic is fragrant but not burning. Throw in the Parmesan, nutmeg and drained linguine. Remove the pan from the heat, add a few splashes of reserved cooking water then keep stirring until the linguine is coated in a glossy sauce. Have a taste for seasoning, you might want a squeeze of lemon juice to brighten up the richness. Eat straight away.

Stuffed Tomatoes, Dressed Freekeh and Oregano Yoghurt

I created this tomato dish for my Summer Series 2023 and it's something I urge you to try when the sunnier months arrive. The filling for the tomatoes is the stuff of dreams: a sweet and salty mixture of warming spices, caramelised fennel and courgettes, capers, olives and lots of fresh oregano leaves. Your kitchen smells divine as these tomatoes bake in the oven and they give off the most incredibly fragrant juices which you then use for dressing a bowl of nutty cooked freekeh – the cracked green wheat that doesn't get the attention it deserves.

You then tear yet more oregano leaves into a bowl of thick, strained yoghurt with plenty of lemon, seasoning and cumin, and it's just the thing for spooning over the tomatoes and dressed freekeh. I can't imagine a summer without these tomatoes now and I'm hoping they become part of your good-weather cooking too.

Serves 2
Takes 30 minutes, plus 45 minutes baking time

STUFFED TOMATOES
3 tbsp extra virgin oil, plus a drizzle
½ fennel, finely chopped
   (reserve the fronds for the freekeh)
½ courgette, finely chopped
sea salt flakes
black pepper
2 garlic cloves
¼ lemon for zesting
pinch chilli flakes
2 stems fresh oregano, leaves picked,
   plus extra for garnish
¼ tsp ground coriander
¼ tsp ground cumin

Stuffed Tomatoes, Dressed Freekeh and Oregano Yoghurt

1 tsp capers
6 green olives, pitted
2 perfectly ripe beef tomatoes
50ml red wine

FREEKEH
120g freekeh
½ cm end of lemon, finely chopped
1 small handful fennel fronds or bronze fennel
1 tbsp sultanas or raisins
sea salt flakes

OREGANO YOGHURT
1 tbsp fresh oregano leaves, roughly chopped
⅛ lemon, zested, plus a squeeze of juice
pinch ground cumin
125g Greek yoghurt (the really thick stuff)
teeny-tiny pinch sea salt flakes

First, preheat the oven to 180°C (350°F/gas 4).

Heat the oil in a large pan then add the fennel and courgette with a pinch of salt and plenty of black pepper. Fry on a high heat for 5 minutes so that the veg starts caramelising at the edges. Stir occasionally so that it doesn't burn, then reduce the heat to low. Using a microplane, grate in the garlic and lemon zest. Add the chilli flakes, oregano, coriander, cumin, capers and olives to the pan, crushing the olives slightly in the pan with a wooden spoon.

Cut the tops off the tomatoes (keep them as lids), scoop out the inside flesh with a spoon then add the flesh to the pan along with the wine. Reduce for 1–2 minutes, or until jammy. Have a taste: you want the filling to be ever so slightly too salty as it's going to season the tomatoes from the inside when roasting.

Line a tray with baking paper then drizzle a bit of oil to sit the tomato bases on. Fill the tomatoes with the courgette mixture then pop on the lids. Bake for 40–45 minutes, or until tender but not collapsing.

Meanwhile, boil the freekeh and lemon in a small saucepan filled with water for 15–20 minutes, or until tender but still chewy. Drain in a sieve to remove any moisture, allowing the grains to steam-dry. Transfer to a bowl then toss with the reserved fennel fronds and sultanas. Once the tomatoes have had their time in the oven, you should find they've released lots of fragrant juices, so carefully pour these into the freekeh and toss to dress, then taste for seasoning.

In a small bowl, stir together the ingredients for the oregano-yoghurt then taste for seasoning.

Serve up a base of freekeh on each plate then top with a stuffed tomato and a dollop of the yoghurt. Pick over a few more oregano leaves to garnish.

Spaghetti with Parmesan and Oregano Meatballs

Thanks to the combination of milk-soaked breadcrumbs, an egg, some finely grated Parmesan and a few pork sausages thrown into the beef mince mixture, these are my squidgy, indulgent, take on the classic. Both the meatballs and the tomato sauce can be prepared (and even frozen) ahead of time, making this the ideal, stress-free supper for feeding a crowd.

Serves 5 / makes 25 meatballs
Takes 50 minutes

MEATBALLS
70g panko breadcrumbs
100ml milk (ideally whole)
50g Parmesan cheese, finely grated
sea salt flakes
1 tsp dried oregano
3 garlic cloves, peeled and finely grated
1 free-range egg
black pepper
130g sausage meat (2 good-quality pork sausages)
500g beef mince
3 tbsp cold-pressed rapeseed oil or light olive oil for frying
500g dried spaghetti

SAUCE
1 × 690g jar good-quality passata
2½ tsp caster sugar
½ tsp sea salt flakes
10g butter (salted or unsalted)
pinch chilli flakes
50g Parmesan cheese, finely grated
Fresh oregano for garnish

Place the panko breadcrumbs, milk, Parmesan, ¾ tsp salt, oregano, garlic, egg and plenty of ground black pepper in a large mixing bowl then stir until the breadcrumbs have soaked up all the milk and egg and everything is well combined. Remove and discard the skins from the sausages, and place the sausage meat in the bowl along with the beef mince.

Wet your hands, then use them to really mix the breadcrumbs and seasoning through the meat – this usually takes about 2 minutes until everything is distributed evenly. Roll into around 25 meatballs, approximately 35g each.

Heat a large frying pan or casserole pot (whatever you use will need a lid) over a high heat then add the oil. Fry the meatballs in batches until they're golden brown on all sides. Don't worry about the insides cooking as they'll continue to cook in the sauce.

Reduce the heat to low, remove the meatballs from the pan and pour in the passata along with 3 tbsp water sloshed around the passata bottle to remove its contents. Use a wooden spoon to scrape up any delicious bits of meatball mixture stuck to the base of the pan then add the sugar, salt, butter and chilli flakes and return the meatballs to the pan. Increase the heat to high until the sauce is bubbling then reduce to a gentle simmer with the lid on to allow the meatballs to cook gently in the sauce for 20 minutes. Stir occasionally to ensure nothing is catching on the base of the pan, then remove from the heat.

Meanwhile, bring a medium pan of water to the boil on a high heat and throw in plenty of sea salt to season the water. Add the spaghetti to the pan, stir regularly to prevent it sticking to itself, then check a few minutes before the pack instructions suggest. You want it al dente – which usually takes around 8–10 minutes. Drain the spaghetti in a colander then toss through the pan of meatballs until fully coated in the sauce.

Divide between plates or bowls then top with the extra Parmesan and some fresh oregano leaves.

Spaghetti with Parmesan and Oregano Meatballs

Sage, Onion and Wild Mushroom Pie

Making this pie with your own homemade flaky pastry and the rich, earthy filling of different wild mushrooms cooked down in sage, garlic and white wine is a generous act and such a brilliant way to spend an autumnal afternoon in the kitchen.

To me, there's something quite romantic about going to all that effort for just two of you, hence the ingredient quantities below. Scale it up, however, to suit your largest pie dish and you've got a hearty supper that everyone is going to love getting round the table for (including any vegetarians). The mash on page 119 and marinated greens (page 124) are particularly good served with this pie.

Serves 2 generously
Takes 20 minutes, plus 1 hour chilling time and 45 minutes baking time

PASTRY
85g plain flour, plus extra for dusting
sea salt flakes
40g cold, salted butter, cut into cubes
2 tbsp milk or 1 free-range egg yolk (for glazing)

MUSHROOM FILLING
6 tbsp cold-pressed rapeseed or light olive oil
2 onions, finely sliced
sea salt flakes
10 sage leaves, roughly torn
3 garlic cloves, peeled and roughly crushed
black pepper
300g mushrooms (I like a mix of chestnut,
    button and wild varieties)
1 tbsp plain flour
1 tsp miso paste
150ml white wine

Sage, Onion and Wild Mushroom Pie

PASTRY

To make the pastry, rub the flour, salt and butter together in a large bowl, using your index and middle fingers and thumbs, until you've got large, rough flakes. (Don't worry if some of the butter remains quite chunky). Stir in a few splashes of cold water then mix with your hands until combined to a dough. Wrap it in cling film and pop in the fridge to rest for 1 hour or overnight.

FILLING

Heat 3 tbsp oil in a wide pan on a high heat. Add the onions, a pinch of salt, the sage, garlic and a good few grindings of black pepper. Gently fry on a medium-low heat for 10-15 minutes, stirring occasionally until really soft and golden.

Meanwhile, using a pastry brush or piece of kitchen paper, brush any dirt off the mushrooms, then roughly slice them. Aim for different shapes and sizes to keep their natural shape and beauty.

Transfer the onions to a plate then scrape out the pan. Increase the heat to high then add 3 tbsp oil to the pan along with the mushrooms and a pinch of salt. Fry on medium-high for 5–10 minutes, or until the mushrooms have softened, slightly caramelised and have some lovely colour. Reduce the heat to low, return the onions to the pan then stir in the flour, miso paste and wine. Simmer for 2 minutes, or until you get a juicy gravy. Make sure you scrape any caramelised bits from the bottom of the pan then have a taste for seasoning. You might want to add a splash of water if you feel like the filling could be juicier. Set aside and allow to cool.

ASSEMBLE AND BAKE

Preheat the oven to 180°C (350°F/gas 4).

Remove the pasty from the fridge and lightly dust your work surface and rolling pin. Roll out two thirds of the pastry wide enough to cover the base and sides of your pie dish. (I use a small oval dish that measures 18cm × 12.5cm × 6cm.) Using a sharp knife, cut away any overhang. Prick the base with a fork.

Cover the pastry base with a sheet of greaseproof paper and add baking beans or rice to weigh the pastry down. Bake in the preheated oven for 20 minutes. Remove the paper and baking beans, bake for a further 5 minutes, then allow to cool for a few minutes. Add in the cooled mushroom filling.

Roll out the remaining pastry to make the pie lid and lay it over the top of the filling. Cut out any decoration you like from any off-cuts, or keep it simple and rustic. Using a fork or your fingers, press all the way round the pie lid to crimp and seal the edges, then brush with milk or egg yolk. Cut a few incisions to allow any steam to escape.

Return to the oven and bake for 20–25 minutes or until golden and crisp. Serve straight away.

Chicken Curry Pie

Where the wild mushroom pie on page 112 is led by consideration for beautiful, seasonal ingredients, this chicken curry pie comes completely from a place of nostalgia as it's the kind my dad would always order for me when we went to football matches together.

A few handfuls of boiled sweetcorn and peas (both from the freezer) for drowning in malt vinegar and loads of sea salt feels right for accompanying it – nothing fancier is needed.

Serves 4–6
Takes 20 minutes, plus 1 hour chilling time and 55 minutes baking time

PASTRY
150g plain flour, plus extra for dusting
tiny pinch of sea salt flakes
85g cold salted butter, cut into cubes
2 tbsp milk or 1 free-range egg yolk (for glazing)

FILLING
3 tbsp cold-pressed rapeseed oil or vegetable oil
2 onions, finely sliced
1 tsp sea salt flakes
650g free-range chicken thighs, skinless, boneless, roughly chopped
4 garlic cloves, peeled and crushed
2 tbsp curry powder
1 tsp ground cumin
1 tsp garam masala
1 tbsp tomato purée
½ tsp chilli flakes
140g natural yoghurt
2 ripe tomatoes, finely chopped

PASTRY

To make the pastry, rub the flour, salt and butter together in a large bowl, using your index and middle fingers and thumbs, until you've got large, rough flakes. (Don't worry if some of the butter remains quite chunky.) Stir in a few splashes of cold water, then mix with your hands until combined to a dough. Wrap it in cling film and pop in the fridge to rest for 1 hour or overnight.

ASSEMBLE AND BAKE

Preheat the oven to 180°C (350°F/gas 4).

Make the filling by heating 2 tbsp oil in a large pan over a high heat. Once hot, add the onions and salt then fry for 4 minutes or until beginning to soften and lightly charring at the edges. Add the remaining 1 tbsp oil and the chicken to the pan and fry for a further 6 minutes to seal and lightly brown the meat.

Reduce the heat to low, stir in the garlic and spices then fry for 2 minutes or until fragrant. Stir in the tomato purée, chilli flakes, yoghurt and tomatoes. Remove from the heat and set aside to cool.

Remove the pasty from the fridge and lightly dust your work surface and rolling pin with flour. Roll out two thirds of the pastry, wide enough to cover the base and sides of your pie dish. (I use a medium rectangular dish that measures 24cm × 18cm × 5cm.) Using a sharp knife, cut away any overhang. Prick the base with a fork.

Cover the pastry base with a sheet of greaseproof paper and add baking beans or rice to weigh the pastry down. Bake in the preheated oven for 20 minutes. Remove the paper and baking beans, bake for a further 5 minutes, then allow to cool. Add in the chicken curry filling.

Roll out the remaining pastry to make the pie lid and lay it over the top of the filling. Cut out any decoration you like from any off-cuts, or keep it simple and rustic. Using a fork or your fingers, press all the way round the pie lid to crimp and seal the edges, then brush with milk or egg yolk. Cut a few incisions to allow any steam to escape.

Chicken Curry Pie

Return to the oven and bake for 30 minutes or until golden and crisp. Serve straight away.

NOTES

+ This pie is best eaten on the day of baking, although slightly soggy pastry leftovers are delicious the next day, too!

Crispy Garlic, Cheddar and Spring Onion Mash

Crispy Garlic, Cheddar and Spring Onion Mash

Inspired by a packet of cheese and onion crisps and with a high ratio of dairy to carbs, this is my answer to comforting soul food. Eat this mash with pie (page 112), sausages, or, when really in need of a hug, straight from the pan.

Serves 2 generously
Takes 20 minutes, plus 15 minutes boiling time

CRISPY GARLIC SLICES
3 tbsp cold-pressed rapeseed oil or light olive oil
4 garlic cloves, peeled and finely sliced

MASHED POTATOES
sea salt flakes
400g baby potatoes
3 garlic cloves, peeled
150ml milk (ideally whole)
50ml white wine
4 spring onions
50g Cheddar cheese
35g Parmesan cheese

CRISPY GARLIC SLICES
Heat the oil in a small frying pan on a medium heat. Add the garlic and fry for 2–3 minutes until golden and crisp. Take care not to burn the garlic or you risk it becoming overly bitter.

Using a slotted spoon, remove the garlic from the pan and transfer to a plate to stop it cooking. Transfer the garlic-infused oil into a small heatproof bowl and set aside.

MASHED POTATOES

Bring a medium pan of water to the boil, add 1 tsp salt and the potatoes (don't bother peeling them), then simmer for 15 minutes, or until tender when a sharp knife is inserted. Drain in a colander and allow to steam-dry.

Wipe out the pan, then heat the garlic-infused oil on a medium heat. Gently crush the three remaining garlic cloves (yes, more garlic!) with the side of your knife and fry for 2–3 minutes until fragrant, taking care that it doesn't burn. Add the milk, wine and drained potatoes, then use a potato masher or strong fork to crush the potatoes until mashed to your preferred consistency. Remove from the heat.

Finely slice the spring onions and grate both cheeses, then stir into the mash along with the crispy garlic slices. The cheese should melt in the residual heat, but re-heat on low if needed. Taste for seasoning, you may want to add a pinch of salt, (or you may find it's seasoned enough from the Parmesan).

NOTES

+ Once you're in the swing of crisping up garlic slices using the method above, it's worth making a larger batch for keeping in the fridge and serving over fried eggs or noodle and rice dishes along with some chilli oil for a quick midweek supper.

Braised Olive, Rosemary and Lentil Casarecce

I've been making this *sort-of* pasta salad for years now as it involves very little faff but contains seriously bold flavours thanks to the olives, rosemary and radicchio. We often eat this midweek using a 250g sachet of pre-cooked puy lentils, but with lentils you've cooked from scratch, some sourdough baguette and wine served alongside it feels special enough for a Saturday night dinner. If you don't want to cook the lentils from scratch, I really like the Merchant Gourmet ones.

Serves 4
Takes 35 minutes

90g dried green lentils
2 bay leaves
200g casarecce pasta (or penne/orecchiette)
180g jarred pitted Kalamata olives in brine (drained weight)
3 tbsp extra virgin olive oil
½–1 tsp chilli flakes
sea salt flakes
2 tsp brown sugar (light or dark)
3 tbsp red wine vinegar
3 sprigs rosemary, leaves picked
3 fat garlic cloves
1 lemon
1 small radicchio (200g)

First, place the lentils and bay leaves in a large pan then top up with plenty of cold water. Bring to the boil then reduce the heat and simmer for 25 minutes, or until tender but cooked through. Drain in a colander then discard the bay leaves.

Bring another large pan of water to the boil. Carefully add the pasta and boil over a high heat, stirring regularly to prevent it sticking to itself, then check a few minutes

Braised Olive, Rosemary and Lentil Casarecce

before the pack instructions suggest. You want it al dente – which usually takes around 8–10 minutes. Drain the pasta, reserving a mugful of the cooking water.

Meanwhile, drain and rinse the olives then add to a large frying pan along with the extra virgin olive oil. Place over a medium heat then add ½ tsp chilli flakes, ½ tsp of salt, the sugar, vinegar and rosemary. Peel and bash the garlic cloves, then add to the pan. Using a speed peeler, create thin strips of lemon zest (avoid the bitter white pith) and add to the pan along with the juice of half the lemon. If the olives look to be drying out at any point, splash in some of the pasta cooking water.

Stir the cooked pasta into the olives along with the lentils. Remove any tired-looking outer leaves from the radicchio, then tear and stir through the pasta. Increase the heat to high for 1 minute then remove.

Have a taste to check the seasoning. Depending on how naturally salty your olives are, you may want to add more salt, lemon juice or chilli flakes. Serve warm or at room temperature.

Marinated Greens

Hardy cabbages and kales might not be everyone's immediate comfort food of choice, but marinating cavolo nero or savoy cabbage leaves in really good cider vinegar, your best olive oil and lots of seasoning transforms them into a really enjoyable side. They're really well suited to the galette (page 55) and mushroom pie on page 112. Plus, they allow you to get ahead if you're feeding a big crowd.

Serves 2 generously
Takes 10 minutes

sea salt flakes
225g dark green cabbage
　(savoy cabbage, cavolo nero or kale work well)
40ml cold-pressed rapeseed oil or extra virgin
　olive oil
black pepper
½ tsp good-quality cider vinegar
⅓ lemon, zested with a microplane

Bring a medium pan of water to the boil, throw in a generous pinch of salt.

Remove and discard the stems from the cabbage, then roughly tear into random, large shreds. Boil the cabbage for 2–3 minutes, then drain well in a colander.

In a large bowl, stir together the oil, plenty of salt and freshly ground pepper, vinegar and lemon zest. Toss the drained cabbage in the dressing where it will sit happily for a few hours at room temperature. (If you like, gently heat in a pan for a minute or so before serving up.)

Marinated Greens

Puddings

Lemon Peel and Bay Custard
129

Blackcurrant Pavlova
with elderflower cream and
lemon peel and bay custard
133

Lemon Posset
136

Forced Rhubarb and Blood Orange Jelly
139

Flourless Chocolate Cake
with crème fraîche and Armagnac prunes
143

Sourdough Summer Pudding
145

Rye Crumb Ice-Cream Cake
147

Cherry and Almond Pudding
151

Puddings

Apple and Almond Frangipane Galette
153

Coriander Seed Crispbreads
for cheese and honey
156

Lemon Peel and Bay Custard

We are big custard fans in this family: hot custard, cold custard, posh 'crème Anglaise' from a fancy restaurant, cheap tinned custard, even lumpy school dinner-style custard made from powder – all are welcome in our house. When it comes to making the stuff from scratch, though, this is the way for me: not overly sweet, but just sweet enough; comforting and familiar, yet surprisingly fragrant thanks to the essential oils coming from the bay and lemon.

Once cooled and therefore even further thickened, this lemon-peel and bay custard transforms a simple pavlova into the most memorable of puddings (see page 133). Drown me in this stuff and I will die happy!

p.s. The blackcurrant leaves aren't essential, they're just an added layer of flavour. We happen to have loads in our garden, but do not worry if you can't get any, the lemon peel and bay alone is perfect.

Serves 4
Takes 20 minutes

1 lemon
600ml double cream
5 bay leaves (ideally fresh, but dried are fine too)
3 free-range egg yolks
   (save the whites for the meringue on page 133)
45g caster sugar
2 tbsp cornflour
tiny pinch sea salt flakes
1 handful of blackcurrant leaves (optional)

First, use a speed peeler to create strips of lemon (aiming for the yellow peel, not so much the bitter white pith), then throw them into a large saucepan along with the cream and bay leaves. Heat on medium, stirring occasionally, until bubbles start dancing on the surface.

Remove from the heat before the cream begins to boil.

Meanwhile, using a balloon whisk or wooden spoon, beat the egg yolks, sugar, cornflour and salt together in a large bowl until completely smooth.

Taking lots of care, pour a few splashes of the hot cream over the egg mixture, whisking constantly to ensure your eggs don't scramble. Gradually pour the remaining hot cream into the eggs, continuing to whisk all the time.

Pour the custard mixture back into the pan (along with the blackcurrant leaves, if using), then heat over a very low heat, whisking regularly, for 5 minutes or until the custard is really thick. Make sure the custard doesn't stick to the base of the pan, this will prevent any lumps forming. Transfer to a heatproof container, allow to cool, then chill in the fridge overnight to infuse.

When ready to eat, scoop out the bay and blackcurrant leaves and discard. Fish out the lemon peel then either discard, or finely slice and add back into the custard, depending on how lemony you are feeling. Eat cold or gently warm it up in a pan.

NOTES

+ If you like, the tiniest pinch of ground turmeric will amplify the yellow of your custard, Just whisk it in when combining the egg yolks and sugar. Go canny though, it only needs the teeniest, tiniest amount.

Lemon Peel and Bay Custard

Blackcurrant Pavlova with elderflower cream and lemon peel and bay custard

Blackcurrant Pavlova with elderflower cream and lemon peel and bay custard

This recipe will forever be special to me as it's the pudding I demonstrated when I opened my Studio in 2022 and feels like a representation of mine and Philip's passions, with him growing the blackcurrants and me turning them into something delicious.

A touch of brown sugar brings a gentle molasses note to the meringue, without compromising how crisp and chewy it becomes once baked. It's then layered up with flavours of British summertime: elderflower through gently whipped cream, bay and lemon peel infused through a wobbly, chilled custard (see page 129), and then plenty of fresh blackcurrants for cutting through the meringue's sweetness.

Blackcurrants can be hard to come by in the shops for some reason, so keep a few punnets in the freezer if you do spot them, and of course, substitute with raspberries, blackberries or gooseberries if that's easier. Tart and juicy is best here.

Serves 6
Takes 30 minutes, plus 1 hour 10 minutes baking time and 1 hour cooling time

MERINGUE
4 free-range egg whites
pinch of sea salt flakes
150g caster sugar
50g soft brown sugar
1 × Lemon Peel and Bay Custard (cold), see page 129
400g blackcurrants, topped and tailed
1 lemon
fennel flowers (optional)

ELDERFLOWER CREAM
3 tbsp elderflower cordial (I like Bottlegreen)
2 tbsp icing sugar
250ml double cream

MERINGUE

First, preheat the oven to 130°C (300°F/gas 2).

Place the egg whites and salt in a large mixing bowl. Using a handheld electric whisk, beat the egg whites to stiff peaks (or use a freestanding mixer).

Combine the sugars in a bowl. Spoon one-tenth of the sugar into the egg whites and continue whisking until the sugar has fully dissolved. Repeat until all the sugar has been added. Continue whisking until you can't feel any grains of sugar when rubbed between two fingers. The meringue mixture should be very glossy by this point. Keep whisking if you're not there yet – it may take at least 15 minutes to get to this stage.

Using a few blobs of meringue mixture as 'glue', stick a sheet of baking paper to a large baking tray. Spoon the meringue mixture onto the paper to make a 20cm wide circle, roughly 6cm tall. Using the spoon, create a few peaks on the surface of the meringue (this is an incredibly satisfying thing to do!).

Bake the meringue in the preheated oven for 1 hour 10 minutes, or until golden and crisp on the outside and slightly soft and chewy in the middle (don't be tempted to open the oven door for at least 55 minutes). Allow to cool completely.

ELDERFLOWER CREAM

Using a balloon whisk and lots of elbow grease (or an electric whisk), beat the cordial, icing sugar and cream in a bowl until soft and peaky (take care not to over-whisk or the cream can become clumpy).

TO ASSEMBLE

Place the cooled meringue on a large serving plate. Dollop over the custard, followed by the elderflower cream then scatter over the blackcurrants. Using a microplane, zest over plenty of lemon. (If you have them, scatter them over the fennel flowers.) Serve straight away.

NOTES

+ If I have time, I like to make the meringue the evening before serving. Once baked, turn the oven off and leave the meringue to dry out overnight with the oven door slightly ajar. As it slowly cools, the meringue will go really chewy in the middle.
+ They're not essential, but if you can get hold of fennel flowers, they make a beautiful garnish and offer a little hit of aniseed that contrasts beautifully with the cream and blackcurrants.
+ The homemade custard is incredibly special in this recipe but if you're short on time, just switch for a good-quality 500g tub of shop-bought vanilla custard.
+ Blackcurrants can of course be switched for any other fruit of your choice. Something sharp and tangy works best to cut through the sweetness of the meringue.

Lemon Posset

If the thought of hosting makes you a little bit nervous then this is the get-ahead pudding of dreams for you. Creamy yet bright and with only 4 ingredients (including the salt!), lemon posset is ridiculously simple to make, will sit happily in the fridge for a couple of days, and is such an effective way to finish a supper. I usually serve the posset as it is, but the shortbread (see page 80) and a handful of fresh berries is particularly good with it, too.

Serves 4–6
Takes 15 minutes, plus 3 hours chilling in the fridge

2 large lemons
teeny-tiny pinch sea salt flakes
500ml double cream
130g caster sugar

Juice the lemons into a small bowl (see the note at the bottom about saving the zest), then pour through a small strainer into another bowl to give you 70ml juice without any pips or pith. Stir in the salt, and set aside.

Next, place the cream and sugar in a pan on a medium-high heat and keep stirring until the sugar has dissolved (this should take about 30 seconds to 1 minute). Once dissolved, crank up the heat and keep stirring for 4 minutes, ensuring you regularly scrape down the edges of the cream to stop it from catching and turning brown. Remove from the stove.

Stir in the lemon juice (you'll potentially feel this is a weird thing to do as it looks like the cream will curdle, but I promise it won't). Continue stirring for another minute or so, you should feel that the cream is beginning to thicken in a similar way to homemade custard.

Divide between 4–6 glass dishes or 1 big serving bowl then, once cool, pop in the fridge for at least 4 hours to chill and further thicken before serving.

Lemon Posset

NOTES
+ You don't need any zest for this recipe, so use a microplane to zest the lemon, then freeze it to use in another dish at a later date.
+ It can be made up to 2 days ahead of serving if kept well covered in the fridge.

Forced Rhubarb and Blood Orange Jelly

Forced Rhubarb and Blood Orange Jelly

It's hard to be miserable while eating jelly, isn't it? Something to do with fun memories of parties as a child perhaps?

I especially love this one for eating with chilled homemade custard (see page 129) to brighten the greyest of January days here in Scotland. You'll see that the first step towards this jelly is to make an almost-compotey fruit mush to strain through a muslin and extract the juice from. The sight of colourful juice slowly dripping into a bowl brings so much joy to the kitchen alone. Of course, use different fruits and their juices throughout the seasons – strawberry juice with a little elderflower cordial splashed in for British summertime is hard to beat, for example, and unforced rhubarb though not as pink is just as delightful.

Please note: I've included the veggie 'vege-gel' option below, but to be completely honest, it's much better with real gelatin – you can't quite reach the same smooth texture.

Serves 4
Takes 20 minutes, plus 1 hour straining time and 6 hours in the fridge

400g forced rhubarb, finely sliced
zest and juice of 1 blood orange
2 tsp lemon juice
40g caster sugar
tiny pinch sea salt flakes
3 sheets leaf gelatine (or 3g vege gel)
cold custard to serve (see page 129)
    or good quality shop-bought

First, place the rhubarb, orange zest and juice, lemon juice, caster sugar and salt in a pan with 50ml water. Bring this to a gentle simmer and cook for 10–15 until the rhubarb has turned quite mushy. Place in a clean tea towel or sheet of muslin over a bowl then tie a knot in the top and hang from a hook for 1 hour to strain the rhubarb juice (if you're in a rush, you can squeeze the juice out with your hands).

Measure the volume of rhubarb juice, then top up with cold water to get to 375ml. (Don't discard the rhubarb pulp, this can be made into a delicious bellini or smoothie!)

Soak the gelatine leaves in a small bowl of cold water until soft. Transfer the rhubarb juice to a pan then add the soft leaves and gently heat. Whisk until it reaches just below boiling point, then pour into your favourite moulds, glasses or dishes. (I use hardy Duralex bowls so if using thin, fine glasses, allow the mixture to cool slightly before pouring in to prevent the glass from shattering!) Chill in the fridge until set, this takes up to 6 hours.

Serve up with plenty of chilled custard.

NOTES

+ If using vege gel: Pour the powder into the strained rhubarb juice then whisk to dissolve. Transfer the juice to a pan then gently heat. Once it reaches just below boiling point, pour into your favourite moulds or dishes. Chill in the fridge until set, this takes up to 2 hours.

Forced Rhubarb and Blood Orange Jelly

Flourless Chocolate Cake with crème fraîche and Armagnac prunes

Flourless Chocolate Cake
with crème fraîche and Armagnac prunes

I used to make a few rounds of this flourless chocolate cake each day when I had Elliott's Cafe as it was everyone's favourite. Being a new mum and running a kitchen service morning, noon and night wasn't really compatible, however, so I made the decision to close the Cafe in 2023.

The intoxicating smell of chocolate wafting from the oven is one that I still dearly miss, so I am delighted to highlight the flourless chocolate cake within these pages. Serve it with Armagnac-soaked prunes, a dollop of crème fraîche or even just a few raspberries and you will be pleasing your guests for years to come.

Makes 10 slices
Takes 25 minutes, plus 45 minutes baking time

250g pitted prunes
50ml Armagnac
    (rum or Earl Grey tea also works well)
200g good-quality dark chocolate, roughly chopped
200g butter (salted or unsalted),
    plus 1 tbsp for greasing
tiny pinch sea salt flakes
250g soft brown sugar
    (light or dark brown work equally well)
70g good-quality cocoa powder,
    plus 2 tbsp for dusting
6 free-range eggs
300g crème fraîche to serve

First, place the prunes and Armagnac in a bowl and allow them to mingle.

Next, gently melt the chocolate and butter with the salt in a large saucepan over a low heat. At the point of being almost melted, remove from the heat – the chocolate and butter will continue to melt in the residual heat.

Next, preheat the oven to 180°C (350°F/gas 4) and use the extra tablespoon of butter to grease a 23cm springform cake tin, then line the base and sides with greaseproof paper.

Using a balloon whisk, stir the sugar and cocoa powder into the chocolate mixture – by this point, it should be a comfortable enough temperature for you to dip your finger into. Crack in the eggs and continue to whisk until smooth and glossy.

Scrape the batter into the lined tin and bake in the preheated oven for 45 minutes, or until the cake has risen slightly. Remove from the oven. At this point the cake will collapse slightly and become all truffle-y and rich. Allow to cool completely then, using a small sieve, dust with the extra cocoa powder.

Serve up with the soaked prunes and crème fraîche.

NOTES
+ This cake keeps well in the fridge for up to 5 days and even freezes brilliantly.
+ I like to eat it as is, but some instant espresso powder or roasted almonds or hazelnuts thrown into the batter is really delicious too.

Sourdough Summer Pudding

Living in the Scottish Borders countryside means that come summer we are spoiled for berries, and this recipe feels like such a magnificent way to celebrate them. Just look at the colour of those juices!

If you've never had a summer pudding before, then berries stuffed into old bread may not sound like much of a treat, but I can assure you it's wonderful and certainly more than the sum of its parts. The magic happens in the fridge when the pudding sits overnight, so be sure to prepare this the day before you serve it. Lots of cold double cream is essential.

Serves 6
Takes 30 minutes plus chilling overnight

175g caster sugar
1 lemon, finely zested (a microplane or the fine side of a box grater is ideal for this)
tiny pinch sea salt flakes
800g mix of raspberries, blackcurrants, gooseberries and redcurrants
1 white sourdough tin loaf (roughly 8–10 slices)
300ml double cream, to serve

Place the sugar, lemon zest and salt in a pan with 125ml water then gently heat until the sugar has dissolved and you have a thin syrup – this should take about 5 minutes. Add the berries, simmer for 1 minute then remove from the heat.

Put the berries in a colander set over a bowl to collect the bright pink syrup. Slice the crusts off the loaf then cut into thin slices. Save 2 slices for the pudding 'lid' then, one by one, dip each slice into the syrup until soaked in juice before using them to line a 1 litre pudding basin. You want the slices to overlap slightly so the berries don't fall out later.

Sourdough Summer Pudding

    Once the base and sides are lined, fill the basin with the berries. Top with the reserved 'lid' slices – you may need to cut to fit slightly – then pour over any spare juices without it overflowing. You can save any spare juices in a jug for serving later .

    Cover the pudding with plenty of cling film, transfer to a plate then top with another plate to help gently weigh the pudding down. Chill in the fridge overnight.

    When ready to serve, allow to come up to room temperature for 10 minutes, then carefully turn out onto a serving plate. Cut into slices then drown in cream.

Rye Crumb Ice-Cream Cake

Technically what the Italians would call a *semifreddo,* this sliceable ice cream containing candied breadcrumbs is something my little family are very into, and I'm hoping you're going to love it too.

You don't need an ice-cream maker to achieve the airy texture here, just an electric whisk and three mixing bowls. Just clear a bit of room in your freezer, big enough to fit a loaf or cake tin, before you get started.

Serves 8
Takes 15 minutes, plus 6 hours freezing time

100g rye bread or sourdough bread
tiny pinch sea salt flakes
25g butter (salted or unsalted),
  plus extra for greasing
45g brown sugar (light or dark)
3 free-range eggs
85g caster sugar
300ml double cream
100g full-fat crème fraîche

You'll need 3 large bowls, an electric whisk, small food processor and a loaf or cake tin – don't worry too much about the size.

First, make sure there's room in your freezer for the tin you plan on using.

Pop your bread in the toaster, as if you were making a slice of toast. Then, using a food processor, blitz your toasted bread into crumbs. Transfer the crumbs to a medium-sized pan then heat on low for 2–3 minutes with the salt to remove any excess moisture that's still in the bread.

Add the butter to the pan then allow it to melt into the breadcrumbs, stirring regularly with a wooden spoon to scrape up any really toasted bits that are slightly stuck to the bottom. Stir in the brown sugar, then stir for a further 1–2 minutes until melted into the crumbs and beginning to caramelise. Transfer to a plate and allow to cool completely. Once cool, you should have crunchy, addictive breadcrumbs that taste like Sugar Puffs!

Meanwhile, grease and line a loaf or cake tin with cling film or greaseproof paper and set aside.

Separate the eggs, with yolks going into one large bowl and whites into another. Using an electric hand whisk, beat the whites to stiff peaks. Add the caster sugar to the bowl of yolks, then whisk until pale yellow.

In a third large bowl (please bear with me on the number of bowls out!), lightly whisk the double cream, taking care not to over-whisk as it can go clumpy, then gently fold in the crème fraîche, stiff egg whites, pale yolks and cooled breadcrumbs. Pour into your lined tin then freeze for at least 6 hours. It'll sit happily in the freezer for a few days or even weeks if you're trying to get ahead.

Allow your ice-cream cake to sit out of the freezer for a couple of minutes before slicing up and serving.

NOTES
+ I like to drizzle the tiniest amount of olive oil over each slice along with a zesting of citrus or a blob of good marmalade before serving.
+ Rum-soaked raisins/prunes are also a good idea in the winter months, as are macerated strawberries and cherries in the summer.

Rye Crumb Ice-Cream Cake

Cherry and Almond Pudding

Cherry and Almond Pudding

Think warm, squidgy Bakewell here; but for moments when you can't be bothered making pastry from scratch, lining a tin, blind baking etc. Just the thing for a Sunday afternoon or evening roast before the *The Antiques Roadshow* comes on!

As per the muffin recipe on page 86, you may notice that I suggest slicing up whole skin-on almonds for scattering over the pudding rather than using pre-bought flaked almonds. I just find your own sliced almonds bring an extra depth of almond flavour and crunchy texture to the pudding – particularly good for contrasting with plenty of smooth, double cream.

Serves 4
Takes 15 minutes, plus 35 minutes baking time

100g softened butter (salted or unsalted),
   plus extra for greasing
80g light brown sugar
tiny pinch sea salt flakes
2 free-range eggs
¼ tsp almond extract (or vanilla paste)
50g wholemeal flour (or plain)
100g ground almonds
275g frozen cherries
   (straight from the freezer or defrosted)
20g skin-on almonds
double cream or crème fraîche to serve

First, preheat the oven to 160°C (325°F/gas 3) and lightly grease a small baking dish with butter. The one I use is a round 18cm enamel tin.

Place the butter, sugar and salt in a large bowl then, using an handheld electric whisk (or a wooden spoon and lots of elbow grease!), beat until just combined. Crack in the eggs, one at a time, beating well after each addition, followed by the almond extract. Don't worry if it looks slightly curdled, just stir in some of the flour.

Throw in the flour and ground almonds, then stir until everything is combined.

Place the cherries in the greased dish then spread the almond batter over the top (this might feel a little awkward so I find a spatula works best). Finely slice the almonds, scatter over the top, then bake for 30–35 minutes or until deep golden in colour and set. (If you're using a thick earthenware dish rather than enamel then you may find it takes a few minutes longer to fully set in the middle.)

Remove the pudding from the oven and allow it to settle for 5 minutes before serving up and drowning in plenty of double cream.

NOTES

+ If using pre-flaked almonds rather than whole almonds that you slice yourself, I'd recommend increasing the almond extract to ½ tsp as the pre-flaked don't give you quite the same nuttiness.

Apple and Almond Frangipane Galette

Although rustic in looks, I can assure you this galette has the flavour of a sophisticated Parisian tart. You can make the frangipane by hand in a mixing bowl with a wooden spoon, but my secret to giving your frangipane an almost toffee-like texture is to keep it blending in a food processor for a few minutes so that it becomes really sticky.

Apples and almond frangipane are just the starting point of course – play with different seasonal fruits and try swapping out some of the almonds for roasted hazelnuts or walnuts for extra depth and complexity.

Serves 6–8
Takes 20 minutes, plus 1 hour chilling time and 1 hour baking time

PASTRY
100g plain flour, plus extra for dusting
50g wholemeal flour (or another 50g plain flour)
tiny pinch sea salt flakes
85g cold butter (salted or unsalted), cut into cubes
1 tsp caster sugar

ALMOND FRANGIPANE
50g whole almonds or ground almonds
30g butter (salted or unsalted),
    soft/at room temperature
70g soft brown sugar or caster sugar
1 free-range egg yolk
tiny pinch sea salt flakes
2 tbsp double cream or milk, ideally whole

TOPPING
4 large apples (don't bother peeling them)
1 tbsp milk
1 tbsp Demerara sugar (the crunchy granular type)
(good-quality vanilla ice cream to serve, optional)

First, make the dough. Rub the flours, salt, butter and sugar together in a large bowl, using your index and middle fingers and thumbs, until you've got large, rough flakes. Don't worry if some of the butter remains quite chunky.

Stir in a few splashes of cold water, then mix with your hands until combined to a soft dough. Wrap it in cling film and pop in the fridge for at least 1 hour, or in the freezer for 30 minutes.

Meanwhile, make the frangipane by blitzing the almonds in a food processor until finely ground. Add the butter, sugar, egg yolk, salt and cream then blitz again until fully combined. You can stop there, but I like to keep the food processor running for a further 2 minutes so that the frangipane goes really sticky and almost toffee-like.

Once the pastry has chilled, preheat the oven to 200°C (400°F/Gas 6). Lay a sheet of baking paper on your work surface and lightly dust it with flour. Roll out the pastry to a rough circle, about 28cm in diameter, on the floured paper. You can use a rolling pin or even a wine bottle to do this, and don't worry about the pastry circle being perfectly round or neat at the edges. In fact, the scruffier the shape, the better.

Transfer the pastry circle – still on the paper – to a large baking tray. Spread over the frangipane, leaving a roughly 2cm clear border all the way round. Core and slice the apples into thin slices (don't bother peeling them) then lay the apple slices over the frangipane. You can arrange them in neat layers or go for the more rustic approach as I do.

Fold the edges of the pastry inwards to slightly overlap the apples, pinching it slightly to create a crust. Brush the pastry crust with milk, scatter over the Demerara sugar then bake in the preheated oven for 50–60 minutes or until golden and crisp.

Remove from the oven and leave to cool for a few minutes before slicing. Serve as is, or with scoops of ice-cream.

Apple and Almond Frangipane Galette

NOTES
+ Don't worry if you don't have a food processor for making the frangipane. Just use ground almonds, a wooden spoon and lots of elbow grease to mix it together.

Coriander Seed Crispbreads
for cheese and honey

The more experienced I've become as a cook, the more I've realised that less is very often more. So rather than making a huge cheeseboard with endless varieties of cheese and accompaniments where the flavours can get a bit muddled, I like to finish a special meal with a single farmhouse cheese, some honey on the comb and these beautiful crispbreads. They have a savoury depth from the miso paste, a touch of sweetness from the honey, and best part: a little pop of citrussy spice when you bite into a coriander seed.

Makes 2 very large crispbreads
(enough for 4 people to snack on with cheese and wine)
Takes 10 minutes, plus 18 minutes baking time

125g plain flour, plus extra for dusting
½ tsp baking powder
1½ tsp coriander seeds
1 tsp honey
125g natural yoghurt
2 tsp miso paste (or ¼ tsp sea salt flakes if you don't have any miso in the fridge)
(optional: your favourite farmhouse cheese and honey on the comb to serve)

First, preheat the oven to 200°C (400°F/gas 6) and line 2 large baking trays with greaseproof paper.

Combine the flour and baking powder in a large bowl to ensure the baking powder is evenly distributed.

Roughly crush the coriander seeds using a pestle and mortar or on a chopping board with a rolling pin, then stir into the flour along with the honey, yoghurt, and miso or sea salt flakes.

Knead the dough with your hands on a lightly floured work surface for 1–2 minutes until smooth. Using a

Coriander Seed Crispbreads for cheese and honey

rolling pin dusted with flour, roll out 2 flatbreads as thinly as possible, about 32cm in diameter and transfer to the lined trays.

Bake in the preheated oven for 12 minutes. Carefully flip the crispbreads over using tongs and cook for a further 6 minutes or until golden. Remove from the oven, allow to cool and crisp up, then serve with cheese and honey on the comb.

NOTES

+ Sometimes I serve these at the start of a meal rather than at the end. I'll either brush them with 40g butter melted with rosemary, sage and garlic; or 40g butter mixed with 2 tbsp cider vinegar and 1 tsp sea salt.
+ Once cooled, the crispbreads keep really well in a sealed container for 2 days, so ideal for making ahead of serving.

Published and printed in August 2025 by

Elliott's
21 Sciennes Road
Edinburgh
EH9 1NX

elliottsedinburgh.com
@jess_elliott_dennison

All rights reserved. No part of this publication may be reproduced, stored in a retrieval system, or transmitted in any form by any means, electronic, mechanical, photocopying, recording or otherwise, without the prior written permission of the publishers and copyright owners.

Copyright text and photography © Jess Elliott Dennison

Design
Maeve Redmond

Illustration
Lilly Hedley

Copy Editing and Proofreading
Gemma Hinstridge

Printing
Gomer Press

Photography on page 16 and 19 by Nina Davidson

ISBN 978-1-0686911-1-9
Printed in the UK

Created by food writer Jess Elliott Dennison, Elliott's celebrates simple cooking and life in the kitchen.

Elliott's Studio, a green-fronted tenement building on Sciennes Road in Edinburgh, is an extension of Jess's home and where she cooks, writes recipes and teaches.

Jess's work is inspired by the produce, colours, textures and rituals that each season brings.

She also explores natural materials, heritage craftsmanship and collaboration with like-minded artists in a pleasing range for the kitchen and home.

Find out more about all things Elliott's at
elliottsedinburgh.com
@jess_elliott_dennison